25 HOURS A DAY

25 HOURS A DAY

GOING ONE MORE TO GET WHAT YOU WANT

NICK BARE

LIONCREST
PUBLISHING

25 HOURS A DAY

Going One More to Get What You Want

ISBN   978-1-5445-0539-8 *Hardcover*
       978-1-5445-0537-4 *Paperback*
       978-1-5445-0538-1 *Ebook*

To my mom. Thank you for showing me kindness, passion, and the drive to chase everything you want in life.

CONTENTS

INTRODUCTION

FEED THE COWS

If you don't feed the cows, the cows die.

It's a great metaphor for building a company, or a life, or a dream. If you don't feed those things, they die, too.

I learned the lesson young, mainly from my father, who'd grown up on the family farm. Every morning at 4 a.m., before the sun even thought about rising in the sky, my father headed out to the barn for the first of two daily milkings. The weather didn't matter. There was never a question of *wanting* to milk the cows. You had to, he'd point out. You just did it. No excuses.

There were never any days off. If you didn't milk and feed

the cows, they died. This work ethic was one of the first things I learned as a child.

I grew up in Central Pennsylvania, in a small town near Hershey called Palmyra. We were surrounded by miles and miles of rolling farmland. I had amazing role models on both sides of my family. I always knew that. It wasn't until recently, though, that I started to think about *why* they were such great role models.

My father's side of the family were all dairy farmers. Incredibly hardworking people, my father himself had been making the 4 a.m. trek to the milking shed since he was a boy. Every single day, and then every single night after dinner. Before the sun rose and after it descended. Day after day.

From them I learned discipline, and the ability to work even when work was the last thing my body or mind wanted to do.

I'm often asked why I decided to join the army. The military had always interested me, but the moment I decided on that course for myself remains vivid in my memory. It was the time my cousin Matt returned home on leave in the middle of a tour of duty in Afghanistan, where he served with the famed 101st Airborne Division.

I remember distinctly the pride and honor he took in his service. During dinner, my grandmother asked him, "Do you like what you're doing? Are you happy?"

He didn't hesitate. "I'm extremely proud of what we're doing overseas. Somebody has to do it."

I realized he was right. Someone has to volunteer. We live in a country where our military is all volunteer, and every year, young men and women show up to serve. No one has a draft number; no one is rounding them up as soon as they turn eighteen and pressing them into military service. Our defense is based completely on the willingness of volunteers to step up, raise their hands, and vow to defend America, and it is an awesome thing to behold.

Matt's visit convinced me that I needed to serve at least four years, that I had a duty as an American citizen to show up for my country.

Both sides of my family taught me the value of discipline and hard work in what I now know to be a really unique atmosphere. They were not super strict, but there was never any doubt when they told me I would or would not do something, that that was exactly what was going to happen.

HUMBLE BEGINNINGS

By any measure, I've been a success, but at every turn, I worked really hard for that success. I graduated college and was commissioned as a lieutenant in the US Army. I served overseas as an infantry platoon leader, and gutted out Ranger School, one of the most grueling and demanding courses in the entire American military.

A fitness enthusiast, I started a thriving multimillion-dollar sports nutrition company, Bare Performance Nutrition, from its beginnings in a small college apartment, to its growth in a one-room army barracks in South Korea. After my discharge, that one room in military housing became one room in central Texas, and has now expanded to a huge warehouse and rocket-fueled internet presence. I've grown from discovering a burning passion in the fitness industry to building a large social presence online through documenting, educating, and inspiring thousands around the world.

I live in a world with twenty-five hours in a day, and I use each of those hours to the maximum.

People often ask me what that means: that I live a twenty-five-hour day.

It's about maximizing your day, your week, your year, or your entire life to its fullest. For me, it meant building my brand after working a full day for the army, often while others were asleep. It meant delaying vacations, putting aside luxuries, and focusing on winning back each and every day (which is also something else we will discuss later in the book).

Conventional wisdom tells you to live as if you have fewer hours in a day. They say to cram everything in as if you only had twenty-three hours in which to get it done. This never made sense to me. It gave you less actual time, and often results in rushing to failure.

I'll never forget the moment I learned to stop rushing toward failure. I was a student in the Infantry Officer Basic Course at Fort Benning, Georgia, working with some captains from the hard-core 75th Ranger Regiment.

I asked one of them for advice on how to be the best leader possible when I arrived at my platoon at Fort Hood, Texas. He pointed to another captain across the room.

"You see that guy right there? When the shit hits the fan, when chaos strikes, *that* guy stays as cool as the other side of the pillow. He doesn't rush to failure, but takes the time to assess the situation, develop a plan quickly, and executes it on demand. That is the guy you want to be."

I realized that the goal isn't to rush, but to slow things down as much as possible, even time itself. We all have twenty-four hours in a day, but it's how you choose to live those twenty-four hours that makes the difference. When I started my business, I sacrificed sleep in order to find extra time. Bottom line, I was in control of the day. I controlled my time, and in the end, I controlled what it was I was about to create.

There was nothing in my background—unless you really knew me—to suggest a future of accomplishment like this. I was an above-average guy, but I didn't stand out as someone who would survive a Spartan test of will and endurance like Ranger School, or start a wildly successful entrepreneurial venture like Bare Performance Nutrition.

I got good grades in school, but never saw myself as super smart. I wasn't valedictorian. I was athletic, but never the stud in sports. I blended in and had a solid group of friends.

I was just a normal dude.

SIGNS

There are many words to describe the trait that has contributed most to my success. Words like passion. Focus. Drive. Tenacity.

Whatever you want to call it, for those who had the inclination to look, it was there from an early age. Anytime I took on a new hobby, I dedicated myself to it with an impressive ferocity. When I became interested in something, I took it to obsessive levels of devotion. I committed to these hobbies wholly, and cleared every other interest out of my life.

For a while when I was really young, it was cooking.

Now when I say cooking, I mean that I would gather my friends over and spend hours researching, experimenting and creating these masterpieces of dishes—usually being some sort of exotic cheeseburger loaded with every topping I could fit between two buns.

At twelve, I discovered construction and all I wanted for Christmas was power tools.

I remember ripping open presents that year and pulling out a table saw, jigsaw, and an electric drill. I built a quarter pipe for skateboarding, wine rack for my mom, treehouses for my friends and—the biggest of all—a boat, which didn't end up floating and is probably still sitting alongside the Swatara Creek.

From there, it was lawn care.

I hung posters all around town and picked up about ten yards. I would push my parents' mower for miles to yards that I cared for during the summer. It was my first "business," if you will, and I was in love.

Looking back now I realize that of all the things I became obsessed with over the years, it was creating that *I was in love with* feeling—whether it was a product for friends, something I crafted with my hands, or a "business" pushing a lawnmower miles across town for thirty dollars.

The one constant, though, was change. These hobbies and passions came and went over the years. My focus would burn white hot, until it didn't. Then I would be on to the next obsession.

This pattern was a kind of training until I found the one passion that has stuck, unlike all the others. When I discovered nutrition and fitness, everything clicked, and I've never looked back.

BEING TESTED

Once I discovered fitness and nutrition, it all fell into place. I decided to study nutrition in school, to ensure I learned everything I could about it. I sought out discipline and adopted a strict routine for myself. I even decided to join the army, knowing that would help get my mindset where it needed to be.

I was twenty-two, and I haven't looked back since I returned from a fateful trip to Fort Lewis, in Washington State.

It was the summer after my junior year, and as a member of the campus Army Reserve Officers Training Corps

(ROTC) unit, I'd been sent to Fort Lewis to take part in the Leadership Development and Assessment Course (LDAC). Known among the troops as "Advance Camp," every summer since 1950 the army has gathered ROTC cadets from around the country for twenty-nine days of intense training and assessment.

Remember, up to this point, I'd never really stood out as being great at any particular thing. But at LDAC, I excelled. I crushed it. It was an amazing experience, and I came home with the knowledge that I'd been tested by the army and found to be exceptional.

Coming home from that camp, I was filled with a feeling of accomplishment and conviction like never before. It was as if I had discovered a confidence inside that was already there, only now it was in plain view.

Filled with this confidence, my next step was clear.

Bare Performance Nutrition was born the next day.

I clearly remember this as the first big risk I ever took, and afterward I never felt paralyzed nor tempted to overanalyze anything ever again. I knew that once I decided to do something, once I'd committed, it was a done deal. I knew I had the ability to figure out the rest as I went.

SEEING CLEARLY

Once I discovered nutrition and fitness, it was as if I were seeing clearly for the first time in my entire life. I'd thought a lot about my life's work, and had changed my mind many times. I wanted to be a professional baseball player (just like every other kid growing up). I wanted to start my own lawn care company. I wanted to be an architect.

I searched high and low for my passion.

When I discovered nutrition and fitness, and through that found my desire to join the military, everything fell into place. I had a clear vision of what I wanted to do with my life. I wasn't blind before, but I couldn't see nearly as well until I found my life's passion.

A MATTER OF PERSPECTIVE

Many people, especially those near the beginning of their careers, can't tell you what they want to do. Their minds are closed in regards to what they can do now and in the future. They have a limited perspective about the things they could choose to do, so it's simpler to choose to do nothing.

Sometimes people are limited by outsiders' expectations of the life they should want for themselves. They think the only way to success is to go from high school to college to a job in that field. I never thought that was the only way to success, or even a good way to do it.

I remember being eighteen and getting ready to graduate high school, and people would ask me, "So what do you want to do with the rest of your life?" It was a ridiculous question. How could I know what I'd be doing for the next forty, fifty, sixty years or more?

I knew I wanted to join the military. I knew that I wanted to go to college. It was all kind of open after that, but I also knew that I would learn amazing things from those two experiences. I knew only what I wanted to do *now*. The years after that would take care of themselves when the time was right.

I'm a firm believer in experience. Place yourself in positions in which you can learn and absorb knowledge from firsthand experiences. These things will mold your perspective on life, and where you want to take yours.

No one ever accomplished anything by sitting still and twiddling their fingers as they *thought* about their passion. There is no substitute for getting out and doing it first.

OVER-COMMIT, OVER-OBSESS

That's the thing about finding your passion, about finding and doing the thing you know you were meant to do. Once you know it, you've got to go all-in. Full throttle.

I talked about this in a video I made not too long ago, "Over-Commit and Over-Obsess." The title of the video describes the steps anyone can take to succeed, once they find that thing that gets them out of bed in the morning, that makes them excited to greet each new day.

Over-commit to what you're passionate about.

Over-obsess on it.

Embrace the things about your journey that are going to be hard, and be ready for obstacles. Be ready for bad advice from people you love and respect. They can't see your vision the way you see it. Only you can do that.

WHY THIS BOOK?

This book is my story. It's about a regular guy who lived a regular life, and who, once he discovered his passion in life, did amazing things.

It's the story of how I found my purpose, survived some of the toughest training the military offers, then built an incredibly successful nutritional supplement company from scratch. It's meant to be explanatory and motivational, and draw on my experiences in the military, fitness, and business worlds. It's an examination of where I am now and how I got here.

And most of all, it will offer some instruction on how you can get here, too.

Taken separately, the concepts I'm going to introduce in this book are not earth-shattering or groundbreaking. But like all the best things, take the parts together as a unified whole, and this book will offer you a recipe to find the same fulfillment and passion in your life that I'm blessed to have in mine.

What this book is *not*? Fluff. BS. It's definitely not another book claiming to give you the ability to save the world. It's not about the grind or the hustle, either. Those are the two most over-used words in the fitness space. So many fitness entrepreneurs are busy building social media platforms instead of businesses, and their grind-and-hustle mentality doesn't resonate with me.

I've never liked those two words. It's for people who spend more time posing for pictures on Instagram than they do building an actual business. I watched my parents' families, either busting their asses on the dairy farm or serving their country in the military; they just put their heads down and worked. There was no grind. There was no hustle. You just did what you had to do. To me, the grind and hustle equates to working without passion.

SO LET'S BEGIN BY EMBRACING THE SUCK

Survive enough tough times in the military, and you'll hear the expression soon enough:

Embrace the Suck.

It means many things to many people, but to me it spoke to developing an ability to gut out the tough times. To find happiness and even fulfillment during difficult times. It's an indispensable skill and mindset. And it's where we'll begin our journey together.

★

CHAPTER ONE

EMBRACE THE SUCK

The mind will take you where your body won't. It's a simple concept, but one few people truly understand, or put into practice. Those who harness the power of adversity, who seek out difficult experiences rather than retreating to lives of comfort, those are the people who will achieve what they want in life. *Embrace the suck* is a bit of a slogan, but it's also a reminder that life is like weight training: our muscles grow stronger as an adaptation to the stress we put them under when we work out.

Life is nothing if not a workout on a grand scale.

ORIGINS

I first heard the term "embrace the suck" in 2009, when I was in the Army Reserve Officers Training Corps (ROTC) in college—from my buddy, Luke.

He was my best friend. We'd gone to college together and joined ROTC at the same time. His initial contract was for the National Guard, so he had to go to boot camp before I even started my training.

It's wasn't a glamorous introduction.

There he was, a recruit gutting his way through basic training. Boot camp isn't the best experience of anyone's life, and even though he's a tough guy, my friend was really suffering and having a bad time of things. One day, he's sitting in one of the porta-potties that surrounded his training site, enjoying a short relief from the constant overwatch of the drill sergeants.

And then he saw it, scrawled on the plastic wall in ballpoint pen: *Embrace the suck.*

To be honest, it didn't seem like a big deal to Luke. He wasn't super inspired by it. But when he told me about it later?

Something clicked.

It struck a chord in my head. I knew it was a military term, but I adopted it on the spot. I've continued to use it in business, in life, in my personal stuff, while working out. I literally apply it to every aspect of my life.

I promise, if you adopt it, too, it'll have as amazing an impact on you as it did on me.

HUMPING FOR HARVEY

First, a word of explanation. "Hump" in military parlance has a HUGELY different meaning than in the civilian world. Ask an infantry veteran about a hump, and they'll tell you a hump is a really fast, really long march, often carrying up to one-hundred pounds of equipment (though the official standard is usually thirty-five for a timed forced march). They usually begin before dawn and end during the peak heat of the day. It's conditioning, to be sure, but also a gut check on a unit-wide basis.

The pace is usually brisk—faster than a walk, but just slow enough to *not* be a jog. Keep it up over fifteen to twenty miles in combat fatigues and boots, a weapon of some kind in your arms (or, like the poor mortar teams, heavy tubes, and plates strapped to your pack), and you can imagine: there's a significant amount of suck to embrace.

Flash forward to 2017. I've been out of the military for a year, and I was getting that itch to just kick my own ass once again. Part of it is to stretch my abilities, but a lot of it also is meant to be humbling, too. The pain and discomfort reenergizes me and recharges me creatively.

I think we all need to find that thing that re-centers us. For some, it's therapy. Others, meditation, or a long walk on the beach.

For me, it's getting my ass kicked over a long period of time. Crazy as it sounds, this is my therapy, my meditation, and it leaves me feeling refreshed and ready to kick today in the dick.

I love long endurance events, whether it's a race or some kind of training or charity event. I fell in love with running not for the usual "runner's high," (which everyone talks about but I've yet to experience) but because it helps give me clarity of thought.

I search out events that promise to leave me a physical wreck afterward. Nothing matters more during these things than to simply drive forward and push through the suck. I'm able to focus my thinking to one thing at a time, which allows me to dedicate the thought energy needed to find solutions or meaning.

To be honest, I believe this is something I learned during my time in Ranger School. I spent 141 days during this sixty-one-day course (which I will discuss later) and I graduated learning a whole lot about myself.

There were zero distractions from the outside world during my extended stay at Ranger School. I had one mission and I was going to drive through anything I had to in order to accomplish that mission.

This is where I learned the true meaning of embrace the suck, but the end state was obvious and I knew what had to be done in order to press forward.

Anyone who knows me will tell you, these events and challenges are the things that keep me moving on a daily basis. They provide me with a clear vision of what I need to be doing, and where I need to be headed.

In August of 2017, Hurricane Harvey rolled in and devastated large swaths of Texas, including a brutal hit on Houston. I live in Austin, so the catastrophic damage there really hit home to me.

I wanted to help. I knew I had a burgeoning platform on social media thanks to my YouTube video presence and other efforts to grow my company, Bare Performance Nutrition. I considered ways I could raise money to help, and I decided that the best way would be to hump from Austin to Houston.

That's about 150 miles.

In the late summer heat of Central and Southeastern Texas.

Embrace the suck? Hell yeah.

Thanks to my platforms, I raised $10,000 before even taking step one on Sept. 9, 2017, with my brother following behind me in a truck as my support team.

Over the next four days, I ended up doing about thirty-five miles a day. Before that, the longest single forced march I'd ever completed was a twenty-six-miler while stationed in Korea. This was a whole new level of suck. This was ten miles longer than the furthest single march I'd ever done, except every day for four straight days.

The suffering began early.

At the end of the first thirty-five miles, I had a litany of issues. My feet were WRECKED—swollen, blistered, and raw. Every step burned like a fire. The gear I carried chafed my hips. I'd taken my shirt off at some point and was now wickedly sunburnt. I'd also let my emotions get ahead of me, so I'd been running the downhill sections and striding uphill like I was back in the army on a forced march.

Waking up for Day 2 revealed a catalog of suffering. My brother poured rubbing alcohol over my blisters to promote their popping, along with the pins we punctured them with. We then layered the soles of my feet with moleskin as protection.

On Day 2, the first mile was the worst mile ever. I hadn't taken into account that my feet were not in the same condition they'd been in during my time in the army. I could feel additional blisters popping. My sunburn worsened. But after that first mile in, good things happened. I found my groove and remembered why I was doing this. I thought, all these people in Houston lost all their shit, and that's why I'm out here ruck marching.

My body became an accessory to my mind, which was pushing forward when my physical self screamed STOP. You learn about the power of the mind when it pushes you to put your body through something like that.

Things didn't improve on the rest of the march, either. Every night, I knew the next morning was going to be worse. There were going to be more blisters. More chaffing. More sunburn.

But my mind was driving the bus.

My body wanted to quit, but my mind wouldn't allow it.

I thrive on this feeling. I love pushing my body to this place. ENDURE is the root of the word "endurance," which I love so much. Endure the struggle, the pain, and the GROWTH that you are about to be overwhelmed with.

To honor the people who sacrificed so much on 9/11—the third day of my march, which had reached new heights of misery—I carried an American flag over my shoulder the entire day. It wasn't something I did to create an impact, but this was Texas and I walked down the side of a major highway that day. People stopped me left and right. "Why are you doing this?" they'd ask.

Whenever I told them, they'd invariably contribute to

the cause. People gave money. They brought me water bottles. Food. Truck drivers pulled over simply to say "thanks," or to tell me they'd served, too. People wanted to join me. A few offered to go home, get their own rucks, and come out with me. I have never experienced that level of support in my entire life.

If I'd depended on my physical strength alone, none of it would have occurred. My mind pushed my body. I embraced the suck and found joy.

LAST DAY ON THE MARCH TO HOUSTON

I had to get off the highway the day I marched into Houston. The highways were too busy, so I finished the march on the side roads and surface streets of the city. I found myself walking through the neighborhoods most hard-hit by Harvey. Residents had begun digging out by then, and most of the houses were skeletons of their former selves, with water-soaked drywall torn away and awaiting replacement, leaving the studs underneath exposed.

The wet drywall and insulation and other discarded items from each of these homes were piled along the streets, and as I passed I felt as if I walked through a war zone. It was like a ghost town, all these wrecked and damaged houses.

Walking through the destruction was an eerie feeling. I'd

enjoyed the feeling of raising money for these people. But being there, seeing the crazy shit that the storm and flood had done to their homes was overwhelming. I felt helpless.

What's the lesson? For one thing, be kind, genuine, and passionate. Seeing the people of Texas come together during this tragedy was amazing. I'd seen this before growing up in Pennsylvania around the single kindest person I've ever known—my mother.

She was the definition of selfless.

Not many people in the world discover their life's passion early and go on to fulfill it, but my mother did. She fell in love with teaching at an early age, and spent most of her life teaching special education. She even coached Special Olympics and dedicated her life to helping others. My mom was a woman who always put others first.

No one ever had to tell me or my brother how to be kind. We were never told to choose the hard right over the easy wrong. We were never told how to be good people.

My parents just demonstrated those things every day.

My mom, especially, showed kindness to everyone, every day.

When I first started my nutrition company, it wasn't to make a lot of money. It was just something I did because it felt right at the time—it was my passion. The ruck march is an example of advice I'd give to anyone starting out: Be kind. Be genuine. Be passionate.

To anyone just starting out, I always recommend kindness. I learned more while building my business from being kind and really getting to know other people than I did from any other instruction I ever got. Doing that march from Austin to Houston, and the amazing people I met along the way, reinforced for me why I do what I do, why I create content on social media, why I share my story. Growing a business while at the same time helping people as a huge component of that fulfills my heart and mind.

The other lesson I learned was that the mind is an incredible tool when you're focused. I wasn't doing this for fame or money or personal gain. This wasn't a business. If I'd quit, no one would have known except me, and probably a few friends. But I was committed, and seeing the reality of the situation in front of me, the reason I'd suffered and needed to embrace the suck in ways I never had before, that made it all worthwhile.

HOW WE'RE WIRED

Even though I'd served in the army and completed Ranger School, the march from Austin to Houston still hurt. It was one long gut check. If there was ever a time for which there was plenty of suck to embrace, this march was it.

That's when it occurred to me: people are wired one of two ways, at least in terms of whether their body controls their mind, or vice versa. I don't think it's something you're born with, not a trait encoded in everyone's DNA, but rather a mindset that can be changed or evolve.

Person A allows their body to control their minds. These are the people who respond to signals from their body rather than exercise control over it. Feeling, then reaction. They get hungry, they eat. They get tired, they sleep. Their legs hurt, they stop. It's a big feedback loop in which the mind is unable to overcome any stimuli from the body. In the end, when these peoples' bodies tell their minds that they've exerted themselves to a certain point, they stop. They quit. These people are wired so that their bodies control their minds, and if their ability to overcome physical pain or discomfort isn't absent entirely, it definitely isn't well-honed, and will fail them in times of direst need.

Person B, however, whose mind is stronger than their body, is able to drive through pain and weariness, they can ignore hunger pangs and focus on finishing what they started. These are the people who do amazing things because their mind controls their bodies.

This is the single-biggest piece of the puzzle that I've discovered in the last couple years. Ultimately, we're talking about training yourself to make the mindset shift required to be able to embrace the suck, to thrive when times are tough and everything—and maybe every*one*—is telling you to quit.

I am by no means telling you that sleep doesn't matter, or that eating doesn't matter, or that proper recovery protocols to prevent injury don't matter, but come on! I've grown more in my life during times of weariness, hunger, and hurt. I'm not suggesting that these should be your everyday circumstances, but I definitely search them out from time to time in order to grow.

I talked to my Ironman prep coach one day after a workout that began with a sixty-mile bike ride and transitioned into a six-mile run (a so-called "brick" workout that replicates the bike-to-run changeover in the actual race). It was my final training day of the week, and I was exhausted.

He didn't take it easy on me.

"Get ready for longer sessions, harder days, and dark places," he said.

"I live for those dark places," I replied.

And it was true. I am consciously aware of the pain when I'm in the middle of it, but I also know that the end result will be life-changing growth.

If there is one thing you learn about THE HURT during a contract with the US military, it is that it is not AN INJURY. There is a clear difference between being *hurt* and being *injured*.

I vividly remember sitting in a patrol base during the Florida phase of Ranger School getting foot checks by the medics. They would come around in the morning and essentially make sure soldiers' feet weren't falling apart after walking through the swamps for hours.

"My foot hurts," a guy next to me said.

The medic responded with, "Is it hurt or is it injured?"

We all knew the difference and the medic wanted to get the message across without saying, "Are you trying to get out of this shit or are you actually unable to accomplish your mission?"

When you put your body through a brutal metabolic conditioning workout, that hurts.

When you try and break your personal record on a marathon, that hurts.

When you attempt your first MURPH workout on Memorial Day weekend after not training, that hurts.

But when you fall from a C-130 airplane and your parachute doesn't deploy properly, well then you are probably injured.

The hurt is fuel—it is your body's response to pushing beyond its comfortable limits. Being injured takes you out of the game.

Remember that.

For most of us, it's these times of pain, hunger, or exhaustion that our mind—not your body—flips the switch to "on." My training sessions, though, are purpose driven. My goal isn't to "workout until dead." If my plan for the day is a ten-mile run at a moderate pace, I'll stick to the plan. However, some of them are programmed to overreach, to go a bit further than I thought I could go, workouts where your mind is begging you to stop but you can't, because you found it's "on" switch a long time ago and broke the damn thing.

That is the way I live my life. I have purpose behind what I do, and that purpose is structured to push me forward. Sometimes I need to overreach and feel that struggle, if only to remind myself that that switch I broke a long time ago remains broken today.

The first step during these times is to allow yourself to recognize that you're in a tough spot. When things really suck, you need to be consciously aware of it enough to admit "OK, this does, in fact, suck." It sounds simple, but it's an admission you need to allow yourself. This admission is the first step in rewiring your brain to thrive in difficult times. The next step is to remind yourself what you have to do. "This sucks, and now I have to be aware of what I'm doing and what I'm experiencing right now, and realize that I have to live and embrace this discomfort and pain." Embracing the experience of pain and discomfort is the key to helping you shift to your mind controlling your body.

Forget the hunger.

Forget the exhaustion.

Ignore the hurt.

Embrace the suck, let your mind control your body, and drive on.

NO EASY PATH

Some sports and performance psychologists will talk about "flipping switches" psychologically to tap into this mindset. As if you're a machine in which a setting simply needs adjustment and you'll find the initiative and mindset you need to perform under stress and pain. We'll talk more about this switch later, but for now just remember that the switch's presence, and our ability to use it, is often at the heart of why people quit when they do.

Unfortunately, like the most important things in life, there is no shortcut. There is no pill to take, no mantra to recite. If anything, rewiring your brain to embrace the suck doesn't involve forgetting or distracting yourself from the pain. It means facing the pain and discomfort straight-on, and persevering anyway.

You need to be consciously aware of the idea that "this really sucks and I want to quit," and then happily allowing your mind to demand that your body hang in there and soak it all in.

LEARNING ON A LONG MOUNTAIN WALK

My own mindset shifted this way during Ranger School. To understand why this was so powerful, it's worth taking a look at the school itself.

One of the most grueling courses in the entire US military, and among the toughest anywhere in the world, Ranger School is sixty-one days of unrelenting training, testing, and assessment across three phases held at Fort Benning, the remote mountains of Dahlonega, Georgia, then finally in the swamps of Florida. It's completed on very little food or rest, involves large amounts of marching across long distances, and demanding technical evaluations for which students are rigorously graded by instructors, who demand peak performance no matter how tired, hungry, or beat-down their students become.

They tell you beforehand not to enter Ranger School with the expectation of finishing it in one attempt. Lots of candidates "recycle," meaning they have to pause training either for failing to pass a certain phase, or injury, or any of another million reasons. Our instructors let us know that recycling would mean delays in graduation, before adding "for those of you who *do* graduate the course."

I started Ranger School in late February, the date of the dreaded Best Ranger Competition. The BRC is a series of physical and technical events, the winner of which is deemed the best already-qualified Ranger in the world. It also meant that Ranger School stopped for a whole six weeks, so that anyone in my course who got recycled at any point ended up with a six-week holdover.

I recycled after the first phase. I got to spend an extra month and a half at beautiful Fort Benning before reentering, and passing, the first phase and moved on to the Mountain Phase. Twelve weeks in school and I was lucky enough to be starting the second phase.

Which I promptly recycled through.

By the time I arrived at the third phase, in the swamps of Florida, I'd been in school for eighteen weeks. I passed the third phase on the first try, but overall, I'd spent 141 amazing days in Ranger School.

The levels of exhaustion and stress reached in Ranger School are the closest a soldier can experience to wartime conditions without actually being at war.

My first theories on mindset came during a long overnight march during Mountain Phase. I remember it clearly. It was about 3 a.m., and we were traversing a draw deep in the mountains. We'd been on the march for several days straight. I was beat down. Delirious.

Someone started singing *The Star-Spangled Banner*. To this day, I'm not sure if it was real or a hallucination, but I remember constantly asking myself, "what the fuck is going on?"

It feels like I haven't eaten in...forever. I'm sucking. I had this surreal feeling, an out-of-body experience where I was watching myself walk from outside of myself. And then, in the midst of the most bone-deep misery and exhaustion I'd ever had, things suddenly became very clear to me. I became super aware of what I was doing and how I felt. I'd reached a point of no return with my body, but my mind took over and gave me some control over the situation.

I realized my body wasn't able to push itself anymore.

My mind took stock:

There's no more food coming.

There's not going to be any sleep for a long time to come.

My body wasn't going to carry me through.

My mind was going to have to do the pushing from here on out.

From that moment on, I regained control over my situation. I embraced the suck, and my mind was able to push my body to keep going, complete the mission, and successfully pass the remainder of the phase.

FIND THOSE CHALLENGES AND YOUR SWITCH

Finding ways to push yourself isn't just about achieving a goal or checking off a box on your bucket list. The goal of challenging yourself, of reaching for something that seems way out of your reach, or unattainable, is an act of conditioning. Signing up for a one-hundred-mile ruck march, or an obstacle race, or an Ironman Triathlon is teaching your mind to "flip the switch."

I'm a huge advocate of finding challenges that bring you to the brink of physical collapse, hitting that space where you have to "flip the switch" and have your mind take over to push you through. Do it enough and you'll find it becomes a conscious habit—enduring pain and stress, and in the middle of that asking yourself, "OK, my body has taken me as far as it's going to, now what does my mind want to do?"

That's the switch.

I recently signed up for my first Ironman distance triathlon. That's a 2.4-mile swim, followed by a 112-mile bike race, capped by a 26.2-mile marathon. I'll need to move my body for over 140 miles in one race. It's intimidating. It's kind of insane. But I'm excited. I KNOW my body is going to want to give up at some point. My only question is: when will my mind kick in, when during that race will I "flip the switch" and harness the mental and willpower to push through? Because I've conditioned myself so thoroughly, both mentally and physically, I know it's a matter of *when*, not *if*, my mind will step up.

Test your limits.

Find your wall.

Train your mind to break through it.

YOU DON'T HAVE TO KNOW EVERYTHING

When I was young, whenever I was confronted with something I didn't know, I'd try to bluff my way through it. I feared looking ignorant, or like someone who didn't have all the answers. High school, college, the early days of my business—I worried about creating the perception that I was an idiot, so when I didn't know the answer to something, I faked it. I always tried to "fake it until you make it."

My mindset changed when I went to Ranger School. I realized the moment I got there that there was going to be a lot of stuff in the course that I didn't know, and that I wouldn't be able to fake knowing about. I committed to asking questions, asking for help, and admitting when I didn't know something.

Right away, this mindset was challenged. It was while

we were in one of the rock pits at Fort Benning, learning knots. I was learning how to tie an inline bowline knot, and a classmate asked me if I knew how to dress (a fancy way of saying "finish") the knot? I had to consciously force myself to admit I didn't, then to ask, "Can you teach me?"

It was like a light bulb went off in my head, and the results were amazing. It opened doors to accelerating my knowledge and skills, and sparked an urge to learn, to stretch myself. It wasn't a physical kind of pain, but it still represented the "embrace the suck" mindset perfectly. I knew that a lot of the things I wanted to figure out were going to be difficult, and I was going to have to ask for a lot of help. It was going to suck at times, that much I knew. But I also knew it would be worth it in the end.

One of these first areas was fitness. I wanted to know everything there was to know about transforming your body, proper nutrition, and creating the physique I wanted. Like anything else, the best way I figured to do that was by entering a bodybuilding show. I decided to figure this shit out. I knew it would suck, I knew it would be hard, and I knew it would be worth it.

Then I tried powerlifting. A completely different discipline than the kind of workouts required in bodybuilding, I decided the only way to learn it was to enter a powerlifting competition, then figure out how to get ready for it. Where bodybuilding was about reaching as close to aesthetic perfection as you can with your body, powerlifting is all about force, pushing your muscles to get them to move massive amounts of weight. Powerlifters aren't lean and cut like bodybuilders, and getting good at it takes a whole different type of training.

Probably the best example of embracing the suck and learning something new as a way to achieve goals was through my experience with running. I've always been a big guy. I'm not built to be a marathoner, and running has not been my strong suit. So of course, when I decided to get better at running, I entered a marathon.

Embracing the suck means learning, and learning, that burning desire to acquire new knowledge is the not-so-secret sauce to growth in your personal life and career. What happens to unused muscle? It atrophies—loses form and mass and becomes useless. Embracing the suck means you exercise every fiber of your body and soul, and the end result is success and happiness that you'd never envisioned.

THIS IS NOT A HACK

I didn't invent the concept of embracing the suck. When I was in the army, it was an idea we saw everywhere. Whether you are an infantryman in the army, a helicopter pilot in the marines or a TACP (tactical air control party) in the air force, this phrase is well and widely known. "Embrace the suck" endures because it works.

This is not a life hack. It's not a shortcut to tapping into performance potential hidden from the average person. It's a real way of approaching the obstacles facing you, and growing beyond them. We used to say that we "trained as we fight," meaning no half-efforts, no taking it easy simply because we were in training and not on an actual battlefield. Success in life is often like that—you make your own luck, and often that luck is the result of hard work no one else ever sees.

Here's your hack: work hard. Seek out experiences that stretch you out physically and mentally. Learn how to flip your switch. Do a good job at whatever you do.

It's as simple as that.

Flip that switch and break it, so you have no choice other than to maintain and sustain that drive.

What keeps you from being able to fix that broken switch? You have to respect the process. People often talk about enjoying the process. That's easier said than done. Trust me. Sometimes the process is rough, unrelenting, and hard, but you need to respect it.

Instead of bitching and complaining, the "pre-workout" of quitters, just keep your sights set on YOUR goals and aspirations; YOURS, and no one else's.

NEVER TURN DOWN OPPORTUNITIES

Many people, from my perspective, don't reach their goals, or fail, because they turn down opportunities. We hear a lot of praise for the word "no," but I discovered in college, and enduring through my military and business careers, that the word "yes" is even more powerful.

When an opportunity comes your way, you've got to take it. In college, I made it a point to accept invitations to travel, challenge myself, or step outside of my comfort zone because I knew opportunities would open up (barring the presence of a valid reason not to).

In the military, everyone wants to go to the "cool" schools—Ranger, Airborne, Sniper, etc. Those are the badge schools, the stuff that we all kind of thought we'd be doing in the army. But the military offers schools in all kinds of things—languages, establishing drop zones for equipment and paratroopers behind enemy lines, logistics. I advised my soldiers and NCOs (non-commissioned officers) to take any opportunity to go to a school, "cool" or otherwise. They were guaranteed to learn something from the process and grow in the process.

I fell into a rhythm of where, if it was ethical and moral and seemed right, I'd never turn an opportunity down. Saying yes couldn't hurt me. Worst case scenario, I'd fail, but I also knew I'd learn something from *that*, too. People will often wait for the perfect time and perfect moment to try something new. I knew, though, that if I waited for that perfection, it would never come, or would take a long time to arrive, during which, if I'd said yes even if the timing wasn't awesome, I'd have been able to attain ten times the results.

DISCIPLINE

Sometimes, embracing the suck means denying yourself diversions. During downtimes, it's typical for people to seek comfort, whether in parties or movies or whatever it is they do to fill the space between one day and the next. When I shipped out to Korea, I knew I wasn't going to waste my spare time that way.

I'd started Bare Performance Nutrition three years earlier and was struggling to scale, running it out of the small room the army gave me. I knew going into it that there were lots of people smarter than me, who had better credentials, better experience, and who had done more than me, at least in their business lives.

I didn't come to the industry with a Harvard degree. I hadn't done any crazy internships. No one had hired me in a high-profile company. What I DID have was a strong work ethic. I knew the way to overcome gaps in education or experience was simply to challenge myself and work my ass off harder than anyone else.

That's what I did. Talk about a productive nine-month overseas tour.

When I first arrived in South Korea for my unit rotation, I vowed to see this as an opportunity. I had a chance to really scale my brand. While I was in South Korea to do a job for the army, I had lots of free time. Many soldiers spent that downtime playing video games, watching television, streaming movies, or hitting the bars (when we weren't on lockdown), or just bullshitting in the barracks.

Not me.

I committed to spending every waking hour outside of work to building Bare Performance Nutrition. I read books on business and marketing, listened to podcasts, taught myself video editing, photography, videography— anything and everything to build my brand.

I arrived in South Korea making between $2,000 and $3,000 per month with my business. My goal was to hit $10,000 per month by the time we rotated back to the US in nine months. By over-committing, over-obsessing, and sticking to that schedule, I built the brand and managed to reach my goal in just three months.

Now, you may be asking yourself: How the hell is this guy

logistically managing all of this stuff? Shipments going out? Inventory coming in?

A TYPICAL DAY IN SOUTH KOREA FOR ME:

0400—wake up, talk to US manufacturers and handle customer service

0600—Morning meeting with company leadership before PT

0630—Army PT (Physical Training)

0800—Workout and film YouTube videos during the only time available for filming in the post gym

0900—First Call for work

1700—Work Day concludes

1730—Grab my camera equipment and film more YouTube videos

1900—Dinner

1930—More filming YouTube videos and begin editing

2100—Watch online courses on digital marketing, branding, and social media

2300—Write handwritten thank-you cards for customers who placed orders that day

2400—Finish YouTube filming and editing, then upload for release the next day

0030—Sleep

When I left with my unit for South Korea, I needed someone I could trust to fulfill orders and packages. From the beginning, my dad and brother were always willing to step up and help out. They would take over while I was in the field for a month at a time, or they stepped up while I was at Ranger School for 141 days. I could always count on them any day I needed help.

My family was my biggest supporter while building Bare Performance Nutrition. When I first arrived in South Korea, we were shipping between thirty to fifty orders a month. After the first ninety days, we were processing between 170-200 orders a month.

This increase in volume forced my brother, Preston, to quit his job (that he started about six months prior after graduating college) to be part of Bare Performance Nutrition. Even though I couldn't afford to pay him at the time, he believed in the vision and was willing to move to Texas from Pennsylvania to keep the momentum moving.

The Bare family believes in hard work, building the American dream, and good old-fashioned discipline.

That discipline continues today. I continue to challenge myself with new experiences because I know, whenever I do those things, they never hurt me. They only make me better, both physically and mentally.

Once I accepted that I was entering a competitive environment without all the credentials some of my competitors possessed, I had to ask myself, how do I get better? My answer: do more shitty things to make me a stronger person. In short, embrace the suck. I've always valued practical experience over book learning. Whenever I talk to someone, I can tell right away as to whether they're talking from experience, or from something they read in a book, or saw on a video, but have never actually experienced themselves. I never wanted to be that guy.

WORK HARDER *AND* SMARTER

We've all heard that old saying, "Don't work harder. Work smarter!" It's reassuring for all the wrong reasons. It suggests that the main goal in life is to find the easy way, to skip out on hard work and struggle and to hack your way to achieve your goals.

Repeat after me: there are no shortcuts.

Not for the stuff that really matters, anyway. Working smart is always a good idea (it never pays to be a dummy) but I'd prefer to work harder in most cases, because I know I'm going to get my ass kicked. It's going to hurt, and I'm going to experience pain and struggle, but I'm going to learn a whole lot more from the journey. I'm going to have stories to tell afterward that can help other people, too. Having stories to apply to experience gives you a great reference point. They form the foundation of the world you're creating, and they represent knowledge that can never be taken from you. Struggle and stories add depth to your experience, and in the end, will make you more successful than you ever imagined.

DON'T FEAR INEFFICIENCY

There are times to be ruthlessly efficient. When peoples' lives are at stake, for sure. As a general principle, though, I think it's OK to be inefficient at times. That's another way you learn.

Building my business, I wasted tens of thousands of dollars, and thousands of hours, doing things that turned out to be dead ends, or outright mistakes. I rarely proceeded from Point A directly to Point B. To get where we are today, successful, thriving, and growing, was a long, circuitous trip. I made a lot of mistakes, but in the making, I paid attention, learned, and won't make the same mistake again.

Over the years, I've had conversations with well-meaning folks who wanted to focus on the things I've done wrong in building the business. They wanted to point out the inefficiencies in the process, the things we did wrong, and to offer solutions to do a better job. Usually, though, these aren't people who've actually done what I've attempted to do, namely, grow a business from scratch. It's easy to analyze mistakes, but those mistakes were part of my process. Those were the things I had to go through to get where I wanted to be. Don't be afraid to make your own mistakes, either. Creation is messy. Following a dream isn't always a straight line. The only real sin would be to make mistakes and not learn from them.

BOTTOM LINE

Find the next challenge. Don't avoid them, embrace them. See the struggle for what it is—an opportunity to grow, to create something amazing and fulfilling and kick-ass. Search those challenges out.

Don't avoid them. Whenever I try to avoid challenges, it anchors me firmly in my safe zone, doing the things I've always done, ensuring that I minimize pain and discomfort and the chance of failure.

It's a trap.

No one grows in their safe zone. It's a static place. No change, no evolution, no learning.

When you search for those things that are really hard, those things that really suck (like a four-day, 150-mile ruck march in the heat of late summer Texas), and embrace them, you'll have those life-changing experiences that will lead you exactly where you want to be.

The payoff might take two years or two days. Some challenges are bigger than others. But the payoff will always be there, if you face those challenges head-on.

IF IT WERE EASY...

Now that we've talked about embracing the suck, or how to learn and grow not just through adversity, but because of it, in this next chapter we'll face another reality: if it were easy, anyone could do it.

CHAPTER TWO

★

IF IT WERE EASY, ANYONE COULD DO IT

Many decisions in life aren't black and white. There's a gray area in the middle between what you should do, and what's not going to work out well in the long run. It's hard to know whether a project or a business or a relationship is going to end up the way you envisioned it when you started.

The journey can be tough.

But like my father, who worked on a dairy farm as a young man (a backbreaking commitment, no matter who you are), often said, "If it were easy, anyone could do it."

It wasn't always a saying I wanted to hear. When I first

decided I wanted to start Bare Performance Nutrition, I was in ROTC. I'd come home from this military summer training, bursting with confidence, and determined to follow this path that was so clear to me. My big plan was to create a nutrition product, then send it to be reviewed by fitness experts with a major YouTube presence. That was the plan. I figured they'd review the product on their channels and anyone who saw it would be compelled to buy it.

That was my plan. I explained it to my father.

"I'm going to make a million dollars this year," I said. "I crunched the numbers. I bought x amount of product and I'm going to send it to x number of YouTubers, and they get this many views. At least 50 percent of viewers. I'm going to make a million dollars this year. It's too easy."

He laughed. And then he said it. "If it were that easy, everyone would do it."

RISING TO THE CHALLENGE

To this day, he breaks that one out. A lot. He's a great sounding board for any of my plans. He's naturally skeptical, which I think stems from his life on a dairy farm. Things are almost never as easy as they appear.

It was great motivation, and continues to be to this day. He wasn't trying to get me to forget my dreams. When I came home from that army training in the summer of 2012, full of energy and confidence, one thing I didn't have was an appreciation for how hard and long a journey it was going to be to turn my idea into the company it is today. My father understood.

At the time, though, it hurt when he said that. For a moment, it made me worry, "no one believes in me. I'm the only person who believes in this idea." My reaction was one of, "I'm going to show him."

To this day, people ask me how in the world a broke, twenty-two-year-old college kid found enough money to start a sports nutrition company.

In our last year of ROTC, the military-associated bank USAA offered a loan to all cadets. It had a $25,000 limit, and predictably most of my colleagues used the money to buy cars, computers, vacations, or engagement rings before they headed off for army service. The best part of the so-called pre-commissioning loan was that the first payment was not due until six months after commissioning, which was about a year and a half after getting the money itself.

For me this was the Golden Ticket.

I naively thought $20,000 was more than enough money to start a product-based business, and that I'd have the brand fully built before the first payment was due in eighteen months.

There was one hitch. In order to get the money, you had to convince the head of the military science department at the college that you had good plans for it. I briefed Lieutenant Colonel Meyer on my plans to start a nutrition company. I told him where I was having the products manufactured, how much it cost, the marketing plan for the company, and how I would hit a million dollars in sales quickly.

He had lots of questions but ultimately approved the request. A few weeks later, I had $20,000 in my bank, ready to purchase inventory.

I had no clue what I was doing, but I was all-in. I had no background in business. I didn't understand cash flow, and my plan was to figure it out as I went. A buddy of mine built the website, while another friend designed our first labels. I also dieted and cut down to be ready for a photoshoot to help promote our products on the website.

I became the Swiss Army knife of Bare Performance Nutrition.

Meanwhile, I was going to school for nutrition, which

wasn't exactly meeting my needs. The course covered a lot of things like managing diabetes and cardiovascular disease. These are important and great areas for study, but I needed to understand nutrition for bodybuilders. For that information, I tapped a natural pro at my local gym (meaning he made all of his gains without the use of anabolic, or muscle-building substances, aka Performance Enhancing Drugs, or PEDs).

FIGURING IT OUT ON THE FLY

He didn't disappoint.

"Hey man, I've got this photoshoot coming up for this company I've started," I said. "Can you help me lean out?"

I needed to lose a significant amount of weight in the next two weeks, in order to be shredded within a month. He agreed to help. Sometimes, you should be careful what you ask for. This pro put me on a hardcore diet of just green beans and chicken. I began a killer workout routine and cut out everything from my menu that wasn't on his recommended diet.

Up until that point in my life, it was one of the most challenging months ever. I was throwing the weights constantly. Going to college. Trying to perform my best in ROTC while running six to eight miles almost every day.

The day of the shoot, I was on water and sodium depletion. Looking back on it now, I can only laugh. The "pro" information was all "bro-science" and quack nonsense, and the complete opposite of what I should have been doing to prepare. The theory at the time was to reduce water and sodium intake in order to bring a more lean and dry approach to the photoshoot.

The truth: I didn't give myself nearly enough time to get lean, and came into the day feeling dehydrated. I looked okay, but I felt like shit. I was just a mess.

To make matters worse, I decided to get a spray tan because I thought "that's what the pros do, right?" I booked a tanning booth in a parlor forty-five minutes away in Pittsburgh because I didn't want to be caught at a tanning salon near the college. I showed up on time for the appointment and a young woman directed me to a back room, and told me to get undressed.

Now, this was the first time in my life I'd ever gotten a spray tan. I was clueless. So I followed her directions and got undressed. ALL THE WAY undressed. I waited in that room, buck naked, expecting someone to spray me down from head to toe. Of course, the room was cold as hell.

Another young woman came into the room, probably to

give her twentieth spray tan of the day. She took one look at me and screamed in horror.

"Sir! We have a strict bottoms policy here! You must be wearing bottoms to cover yourself!"

Off to a great start.

The next day I went to a gym that I didn't normally train at, paid the owner $100 for allowing us to take over a section of the gym and hang special lighting, then worked my way awkwardly through a series of poses. I had no clue what I was doing, but what choice did I have?

Arnold makes it look so damn easy.

Everything we did was very amateur, but it's all we could do. We had no money. I had no experience. I had no idea what I was doing, but I was passionate and determined to do whatever I had to do to make it happen.

I had no money to hire help for things like shipping and order reconciliation. I managed the website. I placed the purchase orders. I packaged and shipped all our products. I was doing everything, every part of running the company.

THEN THINGS GO WRONG

Everything was up and running. I had $20,000 worth of inventory waiting to be sent to the buyers who would surely flood my website once the YouTubers I'd sent samples to posted their rave reviews.

Except, at first, things didn't quite work out that way.

Only about a quarter of the YouTubers that I sent samples to actually mentioned them on their channels. The in-depth, informative, thoughtful reviews I expected never happened. Instead, the best I got were little blurbs to the effect of, "Hey, this guy sent me some stuff. It's pretty cool. Check it out."

Not bad, but not nearly what I wanted. Or needed.

The website went live and instantly our sales soared to... zero. Nothing. Nada. Zilch.

Holy shit, I thought to myself. I had all this inventory and a loan to repay. Worst of all, it was proving my dad right. I could not accept failure. But that's what my company seemed destined for—abject failure.

I was storing the inventory and shipping it out of my tiny college apartment. You know, the one above the bar on Philadelphia Street in my little college town. The one that got broken into all the time. The one my bike got stolen from. It was probably one-hundred square feet in total. The lock was a padlock affixed to a hasp on the outside of the door.

I'd stumbled on the idea of pitching my products to family and friends for steep discounts, usually at least 50 percent. It wasn't the money I expected, but at least I was shipping orders and moving a little inventory. I'd pack the boxes at night in that room, then drop them in the mail as I bicycled to class the next morning. (At least until my bike was stolen. From there on, it was all by foot...)

It was not, as you can guess, the beginning of my entrepreneurial career that I'd hoped for.

I'd told my dad I'd make $1 million that first year.

Turns out, we made about $15,000 after offering massive discounts and my guerrilla-type, "need more pre-workout" marketing.

This, I realized, was going to be harder than I thought.

Flash forward. 2016. I'm stationed in Korea, leading a platoon as a new 1st lieutenant, and still plugging away at growing my company. One night, I got to tell my dad some good news on the phone.

"We did $10,000 in business last month," I said.

This was big news. We'd never come close to doing that much business in a month before, and I was feeling pretty good about it. I'll never forget what he said next.

"You know what? This thing might actually work. You might be able to have a sustainable living when you get out of the military. This company could actually work out."

He couldn't help but throw in his motto. Although this time, it was like music to my ears.

"I told you it was going to be hard," he said, "that if it was that easy, everyone would do it. But you know, here we are four years later and it's working. You're making it happen."

It was a slow, gradual build. I started the company a year before commissioning in the military and finishing my last year of college, so I was burdened with juggling both. It was tough. I'd go to Fort Benning for training. I'd be in and out of the field. Then I took four and a half months to get through Ranger School. It was hard to find the time to dedicate to building a brand.

In 2014 I really started pushing on social media, documenting my fitness journey. It was cool watching the organic growth of my social media be matched by growth in the company itself. I saw the correlation.

But there was never a moment where I felt like, "it's about to blow up." It was just such a gradual curve over those four years from 2012 to 2016, just chipping away at it rather than exploding all at once.

I started frequently uploading more videos to YouTube, and when I did, I noticed an uptick in the number of orders. The larger the audience I developed for my social channels, the more sales we got.

Korea was a breakthrough. I found myself for the first time in years with a lot of downtime to dedicate to building the brand. My duties came first, obviously, but every minute of free time went back into the company. I knew I'd be there for nine months. I didn't watch television, I didn't go to the movies, I didn't hang out with friends or spend much time socializing. I committed to spending every free moment building this brand. I read books on running a business. Listened to podcasts. Absorbed as much knowledge as possible.

When I got there, we'd been making about $2,000 per month. That was after four years of work. Quite a ways from $1 million. I came to Korea with the goal of boosting revenue to $10,000 a month. Within three months, we'd hit that mark.

A GOAL IS JUST THE CHECKPOINT ON THE WAY TO NEW GOALS

We'd hit our target, but I didn't stop to smell the roses. By the time we'd hit my $10,000 per month goal, I'd already set my sights on another one. That's how it should work. By the time you arrive at a goal, you should already have new ones in place.

I never let myself think, "we've made it!" Truth is, you're never really there. Growing pains are inevitable. When you finally do get to that next level, you realize that you still have problems. Only the problems now are harder to solve. It's an endless evolution, but also a great problem to be experiencing.

Even now, if we hit $100 million in sales, new problems would arise. I'd still want more. It's not that I want more money to go out and spend, it's just that I love this company. It's my baby, and I want to keep it growing. Growth comes with some pain, though.

It also takes time. So be patient.

YOUR PATH IS YOUR PATH—OR, FINDING YOUR COMPETITIVE ADVANTAGE

When I started the company, we were entering a saturated commercial space. Lots of companies were out there making nutritional and performance enhancing supplements, but not nearly as many companies as there are today. The difference, though, was that a lot of these companies hid their ingredients behind the label of "proprietary blends."

These secret formulas were meant to be the thing that made supplement x superior to all the others. Most companies trafficked in these special blends, and hid their makeup behind fancy, cutting edge-sounding names.

The goal of the proprietary blend is to hide the dosage of certain ingredients in their supplements, some of which are super expensive. The best, most beneficial, and most studied ingredients you can put in a supplement are often trademarked and highly expensive. A lot of our competitors want to include them in their mixes, but don't want to absorb the high cost that useful doses of these ingredients would incur.

So they fudge. They'll say, "We're going to have these ten ingredients mixed together in a five-gram blend." Which sounds great, except since it's proprietary, they don't have to tell you how much of each of those ingredients are in that five-gram blend. Consumers see those ingredients in the mix and think they're getting some benefit, but the company that made the product didn't reveal that they put too little of each ingredient in the mix to be of any value at all.

There's a name for this practice: "pixie dusting." It's where companies will include small doses of really good ingredients solely to be able to say the ingredients were in their mixes. It keeps production costs down while making the product look great in consumers' eyes.

After a while, it became clear that everyone in the industry was mimicking everyone else. Everyone had a secret blend all their own, with a gimmicky name, and customers were left to wonder just what it was they were putting into their bodies. This is where I thought Bare Performance Nutrition could be different.

My idea was to make products with no proprietary blends. No pixie dusting. We'd be very transparent about what went into our products. We wouldn't stoop to using mysterious blends, just the best ingredients packaged and marketed well. I figured it was a can't miss idea.

I wanted us to be different. When everyone was trying to jump on the latest trend and marketing scheme, I wanted my company to be known for selling great products that actually benefitted fitness enthusiasts like me.

That's always been my underlying goal, to be at the forefront of the nutrition and supplement industry. The greatest compliment I could ever receive would be for someone to say, "that Nick Bare, he does things differently than everyone else in the industry." I want to be at the forefront of something new and innovative. Not the same old boring way of looking at performance nutrition.

The thing about transparency is that people LOVE it. In the beginning, I was transparent with everything—and to this day, transparency has been a key value that Bare

Performance Nutrition is built upon. I documented the process we used to create new products, sampling new flavors, packaging up orders, and shipping them out. There was no particular reason other than that I needed content for our social media following, so I shared every part of everything with everyone. Transparency worked for us, 100 percent of the time.

We continued the tradition as we grew. If anything, we became even more transparent. I took the audience behind the scenes at our manufacturer's facility, told them who made our stuff and where (Texas and California), and once I got back from Korea, we filmed in our warehouse every single day. I quickly realized that transparency was our competitive advantage. WE ARE TRANSPARENT WITH EVERYTHING, AND PEOPLE TRUST THAT.

Now keep in mind that when I first started Bare Performance Nutrition I was throwing darts at a dartboard, hoping one would stick, in order to find our path to success. As I began to build the brand and learn what worked and what didn't, I quickly realized that there are two very important areas of emphasis that are absolutely necessary: passion and value to your customers.

As I've discussed already, passion can't be faked and it must be lived. As a business owner, your brand is your baby. It lives and dies based off your burning desire to see it through. Your passion must be transformed into a vision and shared with your team, employees, customers, and audience.

By focusing on how to help change the lives of the men and women who follow our brand, who buy our products and who watch my social media content, our efforts as a team moved in the right direction. As we began to grow, the goal was to educate, motivate, inspire, and facilitate implementing changes in people's healthy lifestyles.

I realized, years after our initial launch, that our competitive advantage was the value we offered through Bare Performance Nutrition. If we focus on the customer—how to help them eat healthier, perform better, and train smarter—then we can build a community around the company. While other companies in our market were throwing hundreds of thousands of dollars at paid advertising, we were building an organic marketing strategy through educating and motivating the market.

I understood very early on that we're never going to get better as a company if we're simply doing what everyone else is doing.

PLAN B? WHAT PLAN B?

Early on in the business, well-meaning people would often ask me, "What are you going to do if it fails? What's your Plan B?" This question increased in frequency once my discharge date from the army neared. People knew I had Bare Performance Nutrition, and nothing else.

I had a simple plan.

"There is no Plan B," I said. "I'm going to make Plan A work so I don't have to have a Plan B."

This is counterintuitive to anyone who has spent time in the infantry. Plan B is absolutely necessary. The first thing to go out the window once the bullets start flying, so the old saying goes, is the original plan. In a military operation, you absolutely have to have a Plan B, and a Plan C, and a Plan D, etc. Contingency plans are crucial, as I don't remember a single training event where everything went as planned, or even close.

But in business, I didn't see it that way. My mindset was that I was going to make this work no matter what. I didn't care whether it took me another ten years, I was going to make it work.

The doubters really picked up steam as soon as the early returns weren't great. Things were not taking off as fast as we wanted. Then, instead of asking for Plan B, people would always want to know when I planned to shut it down. "When are you going to shut this little thing down?"

Even our money guy, the accountant, wasn't sure how much longer we could keep the lights on and the doors open. In the third year of the company, we were still only at about $25,000 in annual revenue, and he wasn't optimistic about our chances.

"You should really consider closing this business," he advised. "You've been at a loss for the past three years and it's not making sense anymore. You're just losing a lot of money."

His idea was to close shop and find a traditional job. It really pissed me off. It also lit a fire under my ass. I doubled down. Worked harder. Put in even longer hours, and turned my laser focus on success into an even more powerful beam.

And it worked.

The next year, we did $500,000 in revenue. That was a huge jump, from $25,000 to half a million dollars in one year. Society expects you to be a quitter if things don't instantaneously go your way. I learned the hard way not to listen to the voices that want you to quit.

Be warned, though: once you start something like this, whether it's a business or another huge project that's important to you, you'd better be ready to embrace a lot of hard times, a lot of suck. It's inevitable. There are going to be a lot of shitty moments.

Whenever life throws the gauntlet down, issues you a challenge, even if it's not intentional, you need to rise up to it.

I've seen timelines like this many times before, and I often laugh at how realistic it is:

SEEING THE LIGHT WHEN THINGS ARE MOST DARK

My father's initial skepticism wasn't about trusting me to get the job done. I think he was more worried about what he perceived as my naivete about what it would take. He was skeptical of the mindset that success would come quickly or without much struggle. In the end, he was cautioning me to guard against half-measures.

He needn't have bothered. Growing up, he did a great job instilling in me the commitment to go all-in on the things I'm passionate about. When I find something that captures my attention, I dedicate all my time and energies to it until it works out.

Going into anything new requires the ability to hope. You've got to believe that you have a chance at making it happen, whatever that *it* is for you. You need vision and the right set of skills (in my case, the willingness to learn whatever needed to be learned, and to move ahead even when I had no clue what I was doing), but once you have those things in place, you'd be amazed at what you can accomplish.

A lot of people will see something that captures their attention, and they'll limit themselves, say something like, "Man, I wish I could do that." A wish is only a wish if all you do is wish for it. It only becomes reality when you take action.

That's one of the things that holds so many people back. They hold onto their wishes and keep them as only that. They never take the steps to make that wish a reality. These are the things that separate the successful people in life from the ones who might be super smart, or have a shitload of money, but who don't seem to achieve anything with either. Those who succeed are the ones who had the vision, and who didn't quit when the going got really hard. They drove through failure to reach success.

You want to know how to break free of your biggest or smallest of fears?

ACTION.

Fear will paralyze you. It is like a wall that disables your ability to move forward and overcome it. Too many people allow fear to hold them back from their biggest aspirations or their greatest dreams.

Just remember that the only way to break past these fears—to get closer to your goals, dreams, and aspirations in life—is to take massive action on them and move past these imaginary barriers.

If I had to pinpoint one moment in my life that made me want to write this book...this would be the one:

I was driving to work one morning in 2015, around 5:30 a.m., thinking of a speech I wanted to give. I was leading an infantry platoon at the time and was getting ready to take them through morning PT. I can admit that I was a little moto (aka "motivated," someone who really liked something, in my case physical training) as a platoon leader and I showed up ready to take on the day and destroy the workout.

The platoon's nickname was the Misfits.

A lot of my guys in that platoon did not feel the same way I did.

After that day's workout, I decided to give the guys the speech I'd been working on. It was something I did from time to time to light a fire under their asses. That day, I was angry. I saw so much potential in many of them. They were smart, strong, resilient, and problem solvers, but many of them did not see that in themselves. I talked to them about eliminating the mental and physical caps they placed on themselves to reach levels of success they didn't even know existed, whether in the army or not.

I KNOW to this day that some of those speeches left lasting impressions on some of the guys and changed their lives. I'm still in contact with a lot of them.

I want other people to feel that way as well.

Successful people see the light at the end of the tunnel precisely when everything seems at its most dark.

SURVIVING THE TOUGH TIMES

So how do we keep driving forward toward the light of success even when we seem to be surrounded by darkness and the looming possibility of failure? It was a question I asked myself in Ranger School.

A lot.

One of the toughest schools in the US military, I nearly completed it twice. That's where we'll begin in the next chapter.

CHAPTER THREE

★

SURVIVING THE TOUGH TIMES

Three a.m.

Ranger School.

Mountain Phase. Another long overnight march back to our patrol base and the day's thirty minutes of sleep. Short on food. Exhausted beyond belief. A large part of the Ranger Instructor's (RI) job was mainly to ensure we held onto the guy in front of us, in case we fell asleep while walking. Which a lot of us did.

At this point I'd been in Ranger School for twelve weeks. It's supposed to be an eight-week course (sixty-one training days), but for lots of candidates, that timeframe is purely theoretical. It's a grueling experience, filled with entire days full of pain and misery. There are long marches, intense simulations of raids and ambushes, a constant drumbeat of up-tempo operations often cited as the closest approximation to being in a war zone without actually facing enemy fire.

Many candidates get "recycled," sent back to repeat earlier phases of the course, for a variety of reasons. Sometimes, it'll be an academic or performance failure, where a candidate failed to live up to the standard for proceeding to the next phase. More often, injury and the wear-and-tear exerted on a human body taking part in the course proves to be the cause of many a recycling.

Bottom line: Ranger School is brutal. Recycling just prolongs the misery. I know. I'd been recycled. At the time of this incident, in terms of training days, I'd completed the course and was more than halfway into a second trip around the sun, so to speak. I was tired, and every fiber of my being desired nothing more than to be done with the misery.

Finishing the course, and earning the coveted "Ranger Tab" to wear on the left shoulder of my uniform, meant so much to me. I thought of pinning that tab to my uniform every single day.

In the middle of the night in the mountains of Dahlonega,

Georgia, is where this particular phase takes place. We're stumbling through the darkness, eager to get back to our patrol base and grab those thirty precious and elusive minutes of sleep. The woods around us were so dense you could see the man in front or behind you, and that was about it.

The RIs were struggling, too. Guys kept passing out, falling out of formation in the dark, falling asleep while on the move. "OK, you guys are fucking stupid at this point," one of the RIs said in the darkness. "Everyone walk in a single-file line." It was the only way they could keep track of us at this point.

Then things got weird.

THE STAR-SPANGLED BANNER SAVES THE DAY

From somewhere in the straggling and stumbling gaggle of beaten and bedraggled soldiers, someone started singing *The Star-Spangled Banner*. It started with one lone voice, but soon the entire class was singing into the mountain night. Not just singing. Singing LOUDLY. At the top of their lungs, with a fervor we should have been too tired to muster.

It baffled me at first, but all I could think of was my own misery.

You see, I'd already had quite the Ranger School extended stay timeline. I arrived on February 23, on a day known as Best Ranger Competition Day. If I were to fail and recycle any of the three phases of the school, I'd have a six-week hold at that phase before trying again. That was because the entire school shuts down for a month and a half for the competition, and recycled students get stuck wherever they were when they recycled.

I'd recycled at first phase for failing my graded patrols, thus getting the "opportunity" to remain at Fort Benning an extra six weeks. During that time I got to pull weeds out of Victory Pond, cleaning surrounding woods to ensure they were free of sticks greater than one foot in length, and painted fence posts.

Ranger.

So by the time I got to the Mountain Phase, I'd already been at the school for twelve weeks. Then spent three weeks in a first attempt at Mountain Phase, failed, got recycled, and was now back for a second attempt.

I was shattered. My body was skin and bones. I had nothing left on me. I'd weighed 220 pounds when I started, and by this point I was easily down to 170 soaking wet.

All I remember was singing the National Anthem in the

middle of the mountains, long before dawn, and feeling like everything was going to be OK. I knew quitting was never an option and everything would turn out just fine.

Of course, I had two things going for me from the start.

First, once I finished Ranger School I was headed for my first platoon at Fort Hood. The command that knew it was waiting for me to finish Ranger School before I reported. If I showed up without that Ranger Tab on my left shoulder, it would send the message to the forty guys in my platoon that I hadn't yet met that they were getting a subpar leader, someone who couldn't hack it when the going got rough. No way was I going to let that happen. The Ranger Tab is a big thing in the army and I could not imagine looking them in the eyes knowing I'd failed the course. How would I have been able to promise that I would not fail them, too?

Second, and simpler, failing or quitting Ranger School is just one of those things we each have in all our lives, that one thing that you just know you would never be able to live down, at least not to yourself. I know I'd never be able to live with myself if I didn't finish the course successfully. I decided I would stay as long as it took to pass. It might take me a year, I reasoned, but fuck it. I'll do it.

COMMITMENT

That realization—that I would see Ranger School through to the end no matter what—was a graduate-level education in commitment. It was the first time I really understood the idea of "over-committing" to something. To apply a singular focus and eliminate anything that distracted me from my mission.

There were no distractions in Ranger School. There were no breaks, no days off, no nights out on the town. You were there to learn how to be one of the best small-unit infantry leaders in the world, trained in the harshest classroom imaginable, and that was all you were there to do.

The outside world ceased to exist. When I awoke, the only thing on my mind was, "Let's get through today. Let's pass our patrol. Let's pass this phase and move on to the next one." The few times we were allowed sleep, I'd drift off to the same litany: "Let's get through tomorrow, let's pass this phase, let's pass this school." From the moment I awoke until the moment I went to sleep (if we got any that day), there was literally only this one thing on my mind. No distractions, to the point where nothing else in the world mattered. To this day, that was a foundational piece of who I am.

APPLYING THE LESSONS

Whether it's building a business, surviving a 150-mile ruck march, or learning about fitness and the industry of fitness, this ability to clear my head of distractions, to over-commit and obsess on my goals, these things I learned in the Georgian mountains and elsewhere in Ranger School have stuck with me.

Surviving the tough times is really a matter of will. Do you have the will to put things aside that don't matter in the pursuit of whatever goal or life dream you're chasing? In Ranger School, I'd often reassure myself, "This is tough. Nothing I'll do for the rest of my life will probably be harder than this, mentally or physically. Therefore, everything I'll face after this will seem easy by comparison."

Chasing difficult experiences is part of strengthening that

foundation. Each hard thing I do in my life means that other challenges, especially those around building the business, won't seem so difficult.

DISCIPLINE

Surviving tough times is also a matter of discipline. You've got to be disciplined to keep doing the things you know you need to do, even when those things might be the last things you want to do.

I use the analogy of the light switch. When I started my company, even before the years and years of struggle and especially after I'd been discharged, I consciously flipped a switch in my mind. That switch committed me to the discipline it would take to grow and run this business I'm so passionate about, even when it would have been much easier to shut it down and try something else, or go to work for someone else.

Instead, I flipped the switch then broke it, ensuring that I could never turn it off. I've just kept going. The company is always on my mind. I'm constantly thinking about it. Always hungry for more success. I saw what I wanted to be.

The best thing about a company like mine is that it's a passion that never has to end. Most big things in peoples' lives have expiration dates. Projects are completed.

Degrees begun then awarded. There's a beginning and an end, and after that end you often have to reinvent yourself and find the next big thing. For me, I didn't face any of that. My company has no expiration date. It's given me this forever-fulfilling passion project into which I can pour my time, resources, and money. It's made me very happy.

Discipline is also the thing that gets me going whenever I have a down thought. Some mornings, I'd wake up beat down and unmotivated. I'd engage in some real negative self-talk, things like, "Shit, I gotta pay these bills, and I didn't make enough money to cover them for the company, so now we're screwed." It's easy to fall into self-pity sometimes, for any of us.

That's where the discipline would kick in. It became a matter of, "We'll make it through this. We'll get to the next point. Then the next point. Then the next." Discipline in combination with a broken switch, broken in such a way that it won't let you stop or turn off, have been key to driving forward and surviving the toughest of times.

I flipped the switch when I started, and broke it so I could never turn it off.

VISION

There is one thing those who fail and quit, who don't

break that switch, all seem to have in common: they lack a great vision. They don't know their destination; they have no idea where they're trying to get. Often, and especially in the nutrition space, the companies that don't last are the ones that are merely trying to copy what their competition does. They don't have an original thought in their heads. Their strategy—aka, their vision—actually belongs to someone else, so when the tough times arrive (and they always do), they're not up to the task.

If you do not have a vision of where you want to go, you'll wander every which way, lost and confused. Lack of vision is a huge cause of burnout, too, in my opinion. It's stressful, not knowing where you're going, or even why. You're throwing darts at a dartboard and hoping a couple of them stick. That is definitely not a recipe for success, and surviving tough times is not even an option for these folks.

I say this as someone who made that mistake. When I was really struggling early on with the company, I made all those mistakes. All the shit I've talked about so far in this book? I failed at all of it. That was part of my journey. When I first started, I copied my competition. I tried to figure out only what everyone else was doing, with no concern for what it was I could do differently. I thought, if I copied enough of my competitors, surely something would work. Of course, I was wrong, but learning that was an important step in my development.

Once I really focused on developing my own vision for what I wanted to accomplish, and asked myself what a vision was even *for*, that was when I started seeing success. Once I'd laid out a really specific vision for the company that's when things really began to run smoothly. We knew where we were going and what the next step was. The throwing darts at a dartboard approach disappeared, replaced by planning and executing our vision relentlessly. I knew what I wanted to be doing, who I wanted to reach, and how to make that happen.

When I look back at the fact that I had absolutely no idea what I was doing when we started, no map and no vision, and was still willing to invest all that money to start the company, I say to myself, "Holy shit, I don't know if I'd do that again."

I'd gone into it with a certain amount of naivete. I didn't know what failure looked like. I didn't know what struggle would look like. I learned all of it as part of the process, and damned if it didn't pay off.

Vision is tough and it should not be taken lightly. In the beginning you may have to start with the "throwing darts at a dartboard" approach. Find out what sticks and what doesn't, but it shouldn't be used forever or even for long.

We should all aspire to be the best. In terms of running a

supplement company, if I don't want to be the best then why the hell am I even here? To be second place? Absolutely not.

The goal is to be at the forefront. Be proactive rather than reactive. You will never make it to number one if you are constantly following the footsteps of first, second, and third place.

FOCUS ON BEING PROACTIVE. NOT REACTIVE.

AVOID PARALYSIS BY ANALYSIS

In infantry tactics, they teach you to shoot, then move. Shooting and staying put just guarantees your enemy is going to ruin your day. It's one thing to think a situation through before the shooting starts, but once the bullets are flying, taking time to do an in-depth analysis of your situation, rather than acting and moving, can be fatal.

Same thing when it comes to surviving tough times. It's called "paralysis by analysis." This is when people react to tough times by doing nothing, overthinking situations, and in general watching while their dreams collapse around them, rather than doing something about it. They'll think, "We can't be in trouble, the money has to be there. This has to work in our favor." They analyze and analyze, when what they ought to be doing is working on finding a solution.

One of the greatest competitive advantages I've had, since the beginning, is that I don't get weighed down by analysis. I don't overanalyze things. "I know what I want to do," I'll say. "I don't know how I'm going to do it. But I'm going to get started." I move when I can, figuring out how to solve problems as I go. I am not the kind of guy who's going to get caught short, paralyzed by fear. I may not know how to get from Point A to Point B, but I'm going to get moving and figure it out along the way.

BECOME A LEARNING MACHINE

One thing that I hope is becoming clear the deeper into this book we go, is that learning is at the core of everything I do, and it should be for you, too. I said before that there are no hacks, but that's not entirely true. There is one hack you can put into action that will help you nail almost any goal or hit any target: turn yourself into a learning machine.

CHAPTER FOUR

———— ★ ————

TURN YOURSELF INTO A LEARNING MACHINE

I grew up in a small town in Pennsylvania, and even though the place was a small pond, so to speak, I wouldn't describe myself as a big fish. There was nothing about me that really stood out. Not in school, not in sports—I was just a regular kid.

One thing about growing up like that is that I didn't know what I didn't know. I can remember sitting in statistics class and asking myself, "How the hell do people do this?" Because I came from such a small town, I wasn't exposed to the wider world that much.

I didn't graduate with people who were hungry to start their own businesses, or interested in reaching thousands of people online. Instagram wasn't even a thing at the time, and YouTube was just a collection of random videos. Video blogs didn't even exist at all.

There were people just like me doing amazing things in the world, but I had no idea how they got there. All the businesspeople around me were building brick-and-mortar shops (retail establishments, restaurants, tradespeople), and no one I knew was going into e-commerce.

I can remember the day, down to the hour, when my mind was opened up to so much more. After college graduation, I reported to Fort Benning for a year of training. I packed the few things I had to my name into my truck and drove from Western Pennsylvania to one of the largest army bases in the country, in Columbus, Georgia. I'd always dreamed of moving south, and the military helped me make that move. I took Exit 6 off I-185, found my way to the apartment complex I'd be calling home, got my keys, then sat in my truck for a while, just soaking in all that was to come.

I realized in that quiet moment that I was about to do big things that year. The military was about to provide me with some life-changing experiences and opportunities, and that this was one of the best decisions I'd ever made. Still, I'd broken out of my comfort zone. I'd left home. I'd left my family behind. I was starting a new life in a new state, with new people I hadn't yet even met, in a new job and along a new walk of life.

And you know what?

I was fucking ready.

I was open and willing to take on every challenge headed my way. I loved my hometown and where I grew up. The land, the culture, the people—they're all amazing.

But I had to get away.

I had to find out what else was out there. I needed to change the mindset that led in a straight line from high school, to college, to work, to family. I had to see what else there was and forge my own path.

In that moment, sitting in my truck outside my new apartment, in a town I couldn't call home just yet, I realized that no matter what it was, if I wanted it badly enough, I would make it happen.

LEARNING IS A TOOL, TIME IS AN ASSET

When I started the company, I knew a couple things. For one thing, I knew where to get inventory. I figured out who could make the kind of supplements I wanted to sell, and where to find them. Additionally, I had some idea of how to sell online, how to use PayPal, that sort of thing.

So at least I knew that much.

But the rest of what goes into starting and growing a fitness nutrition company? I knew nothing. That naivete quickly humbled me when we opened the figurative doors to the company and no one showed up. Our sales were nonexistent.

About that time, I graduated from Ranger School (finally) and headed to my first duty station at Fort Hood in Killeen, Texas. My unit was training in Germany for another month, so I found myself with lots of time on my hands and little to do. It didn't take me long to find something to do with that time.

I should mention here that the most valuable asset you will ever possess is time. It can't be replaced, and how you spend that asset is probably the most important factor in your eventual success. Whenever I begin to teach myself something, the first thing I do is prioritize what it is I'm going to be looking for. The information available online for whatever project you're undertaking is almost endless. If you don't go in with a plan, you'll likely waste a lot of time chasing dead ends.

My company had zero sales and no prospect of improvement without drastic change. I had no idea how to tap into the sales channels that would work for us, so I did what I always do. I decided to teach myself how to grow a company in 2014. Taking my last $500, I bought a video camera and got down to the task of teaching myself how to use social media to boost our sales.

NOTE ON GOOGLING

As an aside, one thing that drives me crazy is when people ask me questions they could easily have answered with a simple Google search. For one thing, it's a waste of my time, and you know how I look at the value of time. For another, virtually everything you'd ever want to know about, well, anything, is available online.

To be honest, I've never been a person who would randomly reach out to another person and ask a question if I could find the answer myself online. Take advantage of those tools: websites, podcasts, books, blogs, vlogs, YouTube, all those places are treasure troves of information.

OK, BACK TO THE LEARNING

Early on in my Texas research, I realized that YouTube was going to be a huge part of my strategy. I sought out tutorials on how to put my camera to use and make the best YouTube videos possible for the company's needs. I had to learn this; we didn't have any money to hire a pro to create them.

The other thing is that I knew that I needed to make my own videos because I had such a clear vision for what I wanted the company to become, and how I wanted to portray it to the world. I didn't know how to pass that vision onto someone else for them to create. The buzzword for all this is *value*, providing some form of worth through your social media platforms by educating, informing, and inspiring your audiences.

While as genius as this sounds, it's actually quite simple. I didn't create my first YouTube channel to monetize or sell products. I wanted to create a community and culture around my brand. Growing up in a small town taught me the importance of these two principles, community and culture, and how supportive and encouraging they can be.

I started my first YouTube channel to document and share my journey in fitness and nutrition, and through that, begin to build a community online. I knew it would help the brand in the future, but for the time being, I saw it as an investment, something that would pay off in the future.

I had to do it myself, which turned out to be my best idea yet.

Learning how to make the YouTube videos was what really kick-started me into social media in general. Becoming the kind of person who is self-taught allows your passion to drive how far that learning will take you. I didn't stop with making videos for one specific social media platform. I took what I learned about being successful on YouTube and brought that to other platforms, too.

You have to keep in mind and go back in time with me a little bit for this one. In 2014, the online fitness social media presence was nowhere close to the beast it has grown into today. Online forums were popular, there were a few channels built around educating the viewers, and there was definitely momentum picking up behind the scenes.

I was drawn to using YouTube as my "community resource" because I saw (mainly from a few other channels at the time) the powerhouse it had the potential to be for me. It allowed me to tell a story, document my life, educate the viewers, and most importantly allowed people to be a part of my journey.

To this day I will have people reach out to the team and I saying, "I have been following you since you first moved to Texas." That's the best part. Viewers can go back and watch my struggles, the challenges, the wins and the losses—it's all there.

ACCELERATING IN SOUTH KOREA

When we eventually shipped off for a nine-month stay in South Korea, my learning accelerated into another gear. As I've talked about earlier, other than fulfilling my military duties, every other moment over there was spent working on the business. I was probably the most antisocial lieutenant in my brigade, but I was dedicated to seeing this company succeed.

As you might have guessed, part of working on the business meant learning how to make the business work. I continued to study videography, photography, and social media marketing and engagement. I listened to podcasts. I'd study other YouTubers and see how they did it, how they filmed, their style, how they used dialogue. I'd watch movies and study framing and filmography. I read books on business operations and marketing.

I was building a bank of knowledge from which I can draw any time I need as I grow the business. I absorbed all the information I could find. In the beginning, this was out of necessity. We didn't have much revenue and I couldn't afford to outsource anything. I knew that the only way to grow and scale—especially since I didn't have investors and wanted to avoid a big loan—was to learn.

I describe this as learning to become a Swiss Army Pocket Knife. It's the sole route to success early on in any business. Entrepreneurs in my position need to quickly accept and adapt to the fact that they're going to pretty much have to do it all in the beginning. Unless you're launching with a massive budget or funding, be the Swiss Army Pocket Knife.

I held down all kinds of jobs in this early stage. I was the head of product development, the sole member of the R&D Advisory Board, our customer service department, chief social media content creator, videographer/photographer, website developer, operations chief, logistics chief, and the firm's marketing and advertising manager.

It was a lot.

LEARNING MEANS SAVINGS

I don't think that idea gets enough love. Learning is definitely the fast-track to your goals, but the other point is that learning saves you money. I could (if I'd had any) spent lots of money on business advisors, consultants, brand strategists, professional film and videography crews, as well as shit-hot marketing teams. The business would have grown, but it would have chewed up lots of money.

Learning freed me from all those expenses. By learning how to shoot my own videos, run the business operations, make the sales, market the products, and grow the brand, I became a one-stop-shop that did it all on the cheap.

Free is a kind of cheap, after all.

Learning means savings, but that's also a kind of investing. It wasn't intentional, but the more I learned, the more valuable I became to my own company. I was investing in the brand by also investing in myself.

I wasn't selling a product. You weren't about to find me in a late-night infomercial hocking the hottest healthcare product, payable in three easy payments. I was building a BRAND. Building brands takes time, vision, and a shit-ton of execution. I was determined to be there every step of the way, to ensure that the brand is perceived and valued the way I want.

In a way, I'm glad I had no money. It forced me to add enough skills to be the proverbial Swiss Army Knife for BPN, but I was able to build the brand exactly the way I wanted.

FINDING A ROUTINE

By the end of the nine months in South Korea, I was a well-oiled machine. I'd nailed down and dialed in almost all aspects of running the business. Things were really starting to jell. I'd even fallen into a nice routine.

I'd be out of bed at 4 a.m. There was a fourteen-hour difference between where I was and the manufacturers I needed to deal with in the US. Getting up that early would give me a couple hours before the morning's physical training (PT). My mornings were devoted to the nitty-gritty of running the business.

At night, once my army duties were finished, that was the time I'd get down to the creative aspects of the business. I'd think about ways to help my customers, and try to envision new ways to get the word out about what we're doing. My first step in this process was to go watch other YouTubers and other successful entrepreneurs. I'd deconstruct what they were doing and make my own storyboards of their videos.

That was the connection between the vision I had in my head and the video material I wanted to create but was not yet skilled enough to make. I'd spend this time learning the art behind creating an engaging video or photoshoot or tweaking our branding. I even learned how to code in order to improve our website. Anything that popped into my head became a subject I'd attack with determination. If I couldn't hire someone to do it for me (and I couldn't), then I learned how to do it myself. I was learning what it took to make a great company out of nothing, and it was an amazing time.

LEARNING TO SEE WHERE YOU'RE GOING

The more I learned, the more I began to understand that learning wasn't just about supporting what the company was doing at that very moment, but anticipating where it might go. I tell this to my team all the time, if we really want to be leaders in our industry (and it applies no matter what you're trying to do, whether business or elsewhere) we can't simply react to things.

If we're just being reactive to everything that's happening to us, or to our industry, we'll never be leaders. We'll spend all our time getting kicked around. Learning is an act of will, it gives you the mindset to go to the forefront, to be a leader instead of a follower.

You have to be proactive. If you're not thinking of the future, you're doing it wrong. I'm always asking myself, "Where do I want to be next month? Where do I want to be next year?" Being proactive forces me to evaluate the results of my social media programming, for example, in almost real time. It lets us move fast, anticipating issues before they have a chance to bog us down. Upgrading the website shows me that our product labels are getting dated, so I redo the labels, which then forces me to review our marketing.

As soon as I changed my mindset, when I used the learning machine I'd adopt a proactive stance, that was the year we saw a 750 percent increase in revenue. Learning tells you that it's not enough to know what's going on right now in your business; you need to know what's *going* to happen in your business.

I think that's a great lesson no matter what you're attempting in life. Become a learning machine. Force yourself to be curious, to ask question after question, and tap the incredible resources available online to anyone who wants to look. In the past, information was incredibly valuable, and people hoarded it like gold. One thing about the digital world is that information has been democratized. It's available, cheaply and widely, to anyone interested in looking. There's no excuse for not knowing how to do something. Everything you need is out there, waiting for you. You've just got to become that machine that wants to go find it.

NOT JUST THE COOL SCHOOL

Being thirsty for knowledge, dedicating myself to becoming a learning machine, has had a profound effect on my life, and I know it can for you, too. It used to drive me crazy when I was in the army, leading a platoon, and I'd look at these guys and see limitless potential being wasted because they didn't want to learn.

They all wanted to go to the "cool" schools I talked about earlier. Airborne. Air Assault. Ranger School. All the courses where you come out with a cool badge to wear on your uniform. We had waiting lists for slots in those schools.

But when openings came down for the boring, less-sexy "troop schools?" Not so much. These were incredible opportunities to learn important stuff. For example, I had a chance to go learn how to pack and load our unit's equipment for deployment. I became what's known as the "movement officer." No one wanted to go to that school because it wasn't cool or exciting.

The thing is, I used the skills I learned in that school to learn how to package and ship our products back when the company was a one-man band and I couldn't afford to hire someone to do our shipping and receiving. I learned those skills in an army course, after which I was able to move our unit's over $100 million worth of equipment safely and efficiently from Texas to South Korea and back.

Learning about logistics wasn't the most exciting thing I did in the army, but later, when it came time to set up shipping contracts with USPS, UPS, and FedEx, I already had a high level understanding of how it worked. The great thing about the military, and holding a leadership position, is that it teaches you hands-on experience with managing time, resources, personnel, and money. Something many people never get the opportunity to do—especially at twenty-five years old. The things I learned in that military logistics course, and then practicing on a real life, halfway-across-the-world movement of $100+ million dollars of government property, would prove invaluable once I was home and building my brand.

Seeing all the unused potential in my platoon used to drive me crazy. I'd see these guys, most of them smarter than me, more skilled, with all this potential, and none of them would be putting it to use because they weren't willing to tap into it. I'd sit them down after PT and I'd get angry. I'd tell them, "You guys have so much potential.

You don't realize all the great things you could be doing and learning. You've got all these opportunities here and you're not taking advantage of it." I begged them to go to these troop schools, where they might learn skills that would be worth a million bucks to them ten years down the road.

Part of the reason I'm writing this book is to inspire those guys, and anyone like them. We all have this potential that we can only tap if we're willing to learn. The best move I ever made, and the thing that separates me from maybe more skilled or better educated folks who haven't achieved a tenth of what I've accomplished, was that I became a learning machine. It's an amazingly powerful tool you can put to use immediately.

ENTITLEMENT

One thread that I hope you see running through all of this is the idea that I was never given anything. I had to work and struggle for every single thing I've achieved. It would be easy to see that as self-pity, or someone justifying their current comfort by pointing to what they had to endure to get to that comfortable position.

You know me by now. Comfort is the last thing I'm looking for. I also don't begrudge the hard work. I think that hard work is EXACTLY why I've been able to achieve what I've achieved. It was a lesson I learned as a kid, watching my mother and father every day, leaning into the work that never seemed to end, providing for the family.

Those are old-fashioned concepts, I suppose. Everyone wants the hacks and shortcuts, the magic pill to take or button to push to skip the part where hard work comes in.

In the next chapter we'll talk about the danger of feeling entitled to something. No one owes us anything, and the feeling of being owed is toxic to getting what you really want in life.

CHAPTER FIVE

★

ENTITLEMENT

Even back in high school, I knew that I'd have to maximize the skills I had in order to succeed. I went to a school filled with crazy smart students, or amazing athletes. I was good at those things, true, but I worked hard for everything I got. I envied the people who would get straight As without trying, or who seemed to be able to throw a baseball ninety miles an hour just naturally, almost like they didn't have to work at it.

I wanted what they had. They were just naturally good at everything they did, so good, in fact, that they never really had to work hard at all. Here's the thing, though: talent will only get you so far.

Once you've used it up, or once it's taken you as far as it can, that's where the need to bust your ass kicks in. I look back now that more than a decade has passed since graduation, and most of those folks with all the gifts and talent in the world aren't really doing much of anything. They're certainly not living up to their full potential.

Why?

THEY BELIEVED A LIE THEY TOLD TO THEMSELVES

What lie? They believed the most seductive lie of all. They thought that the natural gifts and talents they possessed were limitless, and that they would glide through life as successful as they were in high school, putting in the same minimal amount of work.

They became entitled. They thought the world owed them something and that it would simply deliver. This is a dangerous thing to believe, because it'll tempt you into sitting still, it will stunt your growth and leave you short of where you wanted to be in life.

That's one thing being in the military teaches you right away. You aren't entitled to shit. Your pay won't change, regardless of whether you worked one hour that day or one hundred in the last week. There's no five-star dinner coming your way. No one is going to hand you a $100,000 per year job. There's no guarantee of a nice place to lay your head at night.

I see this mistake in a lot of college graduates, too. They think a degree entitles them to certain expectations around that first job. So many graduates think because they got that degree, they're automatically entitled to a $100,000 per year job, and it can be so confusing when that's not the case. Forget it if they have to do an hour or two of overtime. The complaining is endless.

EXCELLENCE IN THE MOTOR POOL

My best friend in the army was the gunner on my Bradley fighting vehicle, Sergeant Eric Davis. Though he was enlisted and I was an officer, we shared every waking moment together during my time as a platoon leader and we became close. We'd spend whole days just talking, and I grew to really admire him.

In addition to being my gunner, Sgt. Davis was also the section leader, meaning he often got the shaft, in the form of extra duties related to his extra jobs. Mostly what this meant was that, when everyone else hit the rack at the end of a long training day, Sgt. Davis would head down to the motor pool, which is what we called the facility where we parked, maintained, and repaired our vehicles with the rest of the crews.

He'd be down there for hours, long after everyone else was sound asleep, performing preventive maintenance checks on the tracks and just ensuring that our stuff was always in tip-top shape. It had to be exhausting. I'm sure it was also frustrating, doing more work than anyone else in the platoon. But I don't know.

Why?

Because never, not once, did he ever complain.

Sgt. Davis understood that this was just part of the job, and he was committed to doing the absolute best he could at whatever job he was assigned. Just watching how hard he worked and how he carried himself, it changed my life (and I already thought I knew a lot about hard work). I don't think he'd ever heard the word *entitlement* in his life.

He knew that these were his responsibilities, and he wasn't about to let anyone down. This was my first real job out of college, and learning by Sgt. Davis's example was an experience I'll carry with me for the rest of my life.

This goes for all of my non-commissioned officers (NCO). The things I learned from Sergeant First Class Muniz, and Staff Sergeants Parker, Matthews, and Anderson, were invaluable. They were perfect examples of how to perform your duties and execute all tasks assigned to you with excellence. These men took care of the soldiers assigned to them, looked after them all hours of the day and night, no matter where we were. I learned so much from them, watching them lead by example and own the day.

FOOL'S GOLD

Entitlement is like that fool's gold. People will think that everything's going to go their way because it always has, because they live in the United States, because the universe owes them, for some reason. It's a wrong-headed optimism that tells entitled people that anything they've achieved thus far in their lives was meant to be, and that the future is secure for them.

Soon enough, you see these people later, when the reality of the world smacks them in the face. You'll hear them bitching about their lousy salaries. They'll be pissed that they had to work a few extra hours last week to get a project done. A couple hours of missed sleep and they are all messed up.

Entitlement lets you believe all the great things in your life are just going to fall into place. First, you'll get that perfect job without even trying. Then, the perfect house will drop into your lap, and you'll use the huge paycheck from that dream job you never had to chase to pay for it all. Along with that, of course, will come the perfect spouse or significant other, who will magically appear like everything else in the entitled person's life.

Facing the harsh reality that none of this works like that is a tough pill for some to swallow. As an entrepreneur fresh out of the military, I faced the truth of this right away. I had no job security. The government no longer paid my salary, or my housing, or fed and clothed me. I paid for my own health insurance. Where once the military had taken care of me, I was now responsible for everything I'd need to support myself. I could have felt sorry for myself, or whined about having to provide for these things. But while I was whining I wouldn't be earning money. Before too long, I wouldn't be able to support myself at all.

RESPONSIBILITY

Like Sgt. Davis, I've got responsibilities now. If I don't do my job, I can't make payroll, so my employees would suffer. I wouldn't be able to do nice things for my fiancé. I wouldn't be able to pay for my home.

Transitioning out of the military was a rude awakening—like, you aren't owed jack shit in this world. It was the first time in my life where I had to generate my own paycheck. No one else was sending me one. I had nothing except myself and my business, and anything I wanted to accomplish was totally on me. It was—and is—a heavy responsibility.

The flip side is, I'm not dependent on anyone else for my

success. I can scale the business as much or as little as I want. I can work as long as I want. I knew I was on my own, but I thought to myself, "This is great because I control my own destiny now."

Too many people think they deserve things simply because they are who they are. They'll go hard at it for a year and then give up when things aren't working out as they'd hoped. If I saw the world as an entitled person, I never would have made it. At the end of our first year, the year you'll remember that I predicted we'd make $1 million, we weren't making squat. It was a hard lesson to learn, but I learned it quickly. The world owed me nothing, and if I didn't put in the hard work, that's exactly what I'd get.

Think about the value proposition I'm making to our customers. We appeal to them by offering great supplements at excellent prices, combined with an absolute commitment to stellar customer service. Nothing groundbreaking there, all companies at least claim to do those things, but we're 100 percent focused on achieving those goals. We have to be. No one is going to buy a BPN supplement just out of pity. No one owes me their sales. No one is obligated to part with their hard-earned money just to help me realize a goal. We have to provide them with a good enough reason to buy our stuff, and that's where the hard work comes in.

Even with hard work, there's no timetable. I busted my ass for three years before we had a decent year. And even when we did, I didn't take a paycheck for the first five. I had to put in a ton of work to get to the point where we were making money, and even now, nothing is guaranteed. Entitlement is the ruin of lots of great potential careers and lives.

FIND IT, GET RID OF IT

One of the best things you can do for yourself, and your future, is to recognize whenever you're giving into feelings of entitlement, then work extra hard to rid yourself of that feeling. My personal trick, whenever I feel like I didn't get something I deserved, is to remember all the people out there at the moment who have it way worse than me.

At any given moment, there are members of the military deployed around the world, and their families and loved ones at home worrying about them. All of those folks have things way worse than me right now. There's folks sitting in a foxhole eating a shitty MRE (Meals Ready to Eat) who hasn't showered in a week and is beat down and miserable. It's hard to complain about my problems when I remember all those folks out there at the exact same moment who have it much worse than I do.

The other trick I employ whenever entitlement sneaks

into my life, is I ask myself, what do I want to be doing, and where do I want to go? If I'm not making $1 million this year, who do those earnings depend on? If my ability to earn that money isn't dependent on me, who does it depend on? Can I blame someone else?

Nope.

I am quick to remind myself that it all comes down on me. As a business owner, I reflect often on my time leading an infantry platoon. If the platoon failed in a mission or a task, it wasn't the platoon's fault. It came down on me, as their leader. I took the responsibility for my team. Business and life are the same way. Own your shit. Understand that no one else is to blame for the goals you miss or the things you didn't do to be successful. Take responsibility for your failures and learn from them. Anything you get in life is a direct result of the time you took to get there.

TIME IS ON YOUR SIDE

A lot of entitlement stems from a sense of speed and velocity. Everyone thinks success is a short road, and money, fame, whatever it is you're looking for, is always right around the corner. It can be tough to learn that that's not how the world works.

I understand. I was the same way. I started my company and expected it to be a huge success within the first twelve months. I've learned, though. Whenever I start work on a new goal, or a new project, I no longer look at it as a sprint. We're running marathons here, so to speak. An investment, and like the best investments, success accrues over time. Be patient and don't expect to see results immediately.

SOME OF THIS IS OUT OF YOUR CONTROL

For some of you, the feeling of entitlement may be out of your control—or will simply feel that way. We're raised in a society of helicopter parents who swoop in and make everything better whenever their precious child doesn't have everything they need. When you're never asked to do anything, and everything is brought to you on a platter, it's easy to adopt the attitude that this is the natural order of things. These parents want the best for their kids, but ensuring that's all they get is actually setting them up for huge disappointments.

I realize a lot of the way I see the world is the result of the way I was raised. I said this to my parents in a recent conversation a few months ago. "I really appreciate the way you guys raised me," I said. Unlike some friends of mine—whose parents were always working to get their kids things their kids refused to work for themselves—my parents taught me that you got what you deserved, and what you deserved was a direct result of how hard you worked.

If I hadn't gotten into my first-choice college, my parents weren't the type to pick up the phone and demand reconsideration. Some of my friends had parents who did that. When I got rejected by a college, my mother said, "Listen, your grades weren't good enough." She didn't sugarcoat things, and she didn't make excuses. I learned from them that we're responsible for the amount of work we put in and ultimately for the results we get.

My big dream as a youngster was to play big-time college baseball. I wasn't the best player, but I felt like I had the skills to get there, and I worked hard at improving. My dad even built a batting cage in the garage, and I would spend hours and hours out there, hitting off the tees and working on my swing. I was putting in the work and I told myself, "I'll get there." After all, I was related to my stud brother who chose D-1 college baseball over the D-1 football offers he got. Surely, with all my hard work, the same thing awaited me.

There's no Hollywood ending, though. I worked and worked and worked, and yet instead of big-time college baseball, I found myself riding the bench in high school and getting angry about it. I learned from that, though. When you're playing sports, your success all comes down to you. You can't blame someone else when you don't perform like you need to. It taught me early on that if I ever wanted to accomplish anything, it was going to be on me.

GOING ALL-IN

Which brings us to the subject of our next chapter—Going All-In. If success ultimately comes down to you and your hard work, the only way to maximize your chances of creating something special is to utterly, totally, and completely commit to whatever it is you're doing. Go all-in, or don't bother going at all.

CHAPTER SIX

──── ★ ────

GOING ALL-IN

Near the end of my tour in the army, I bought a small house where I was stationed in Texas, maybe 1,100 square feet. It became the world headquarters of my company. My brother moved in to help me out, as did a friend of mine from college.

Space was short. The garage was filled with pallets and pallets full of supplements and other products. The living room was chock-full of shaker bottles (the special bottles in that include a sifter to better mix the various powders and supplements). We didn't really have a kitchen. It was filled with boxes and boxes, stacked on every surface and the kitchen table itself.

We slept on couches and air mattresses dropped pretty much wherever we could find space. I vividly remember that we had to make a path through the boxes to make room for one of the air mattresses, and even then we carved out just enough space between the boxes in that room for the mattress and nothing else.

Building the company and the brand was the sole focus of our entire existence. There were no distractions. In echoes of my time in South Korea, I'd go to PT early in the morning, work a full day on post, then come home and get to work filming YouTube videos, putting out content on social media, and generally doing anything we could to build the brand.

We skipped meals. Sleep was hit-or-miss. Some days we went without it at all, and regardless, we took as little of it as we could. Then we started building out our first warehouse, which was about forty-five minutes away from Fort Hood, which meant that all the craziness continued, only now I added ninety minutes of commuting each day.

The new warehouse was a project all by itself. Every night we'd be in there laying down rubber mats to protect the floors, or setting up racks and inventory stations, followed by filming for YouTube. I can remember getting home at 1 a.m., editing and uploading the video footage until 3 a.m., then grabbing an hour of sleep before starting it all over again. I was so tired that I'd head in for PT, and instead of showering or eating breakfast, I'd collapse in my truck and sleep until 9 a.m., when I had to be in the office.

That's how I spent my last year in the army and it was fucking wild.

But here's the thing: I loved every minute of it.

This was my passion. There's nothing I wanted more in the world than to build this business into something special.

It was never a grind.

It was never a hustle.

I never complained about the work.

I was all-in, and when you're truly all-in none of that stuff matters, not the sleeplessness, not the cramped living conditions, nothing but the hunger to succeed. Going all-in is the thing that pushes passion and desire over the top.

CHASING THAT FEELING

The mentality I'd learned in the army, particularly in Ranger School followed me when I transitioned out of the military and back into the civilian world. Only now, I had ten extra hours a day to devote to the business. True, I didn't have anything else on which to fall back, so the extra time was there by default, but still. I knew exactly what I was going to do with that time.

The thing that led me forward, that got me to the next level, was that all-in commitment. It's like burning the boats on the beach, forcing yourself to find a way forward and to survive.

To this day, part of going all-in is to chase that same feeling of exhaustion and energy that I felt back when things weren't so certain. My fiancé gives me shit about this all the time. She knows that part of me actually misses that feeling. She knows every now and then I need to go chase it down.

A good example is the time we hopped in the car and drove to New Mexico for the twenty-six-mile Bataan Memorial Death March. It's a fun race, essentially a marathon in the mountains completed with a fifty-pound pack on your back. It was a whirlwind weekend. On Friday, we drove ten hours down to New Mexico, camped out in a snowstorm and temperatures in the twenties. I rocked the race, then we got back in the truck as soon as I was done and drove back to Austin, where I went straight to our old warehouse and continued packing for the move into our new, 10,000-square-foot warehouse. I didn't go home first or anything.

Why?

Am I nuts?

Maybe. But probably not. I'm just all-in, which these days

is generally a platitude, the kind of slogan you can paint on a gym wall but which no one takes the time to really think about. All-in is the epitome of what we talked about earlier, embracing the suck. It's embracing the suck put into action. I didn't need to drive down to New Mexico to put myself through the suck of a brutal race like that, but I also knew it was an opportunity to be uncomfortable, to chase that feeling of exhaustion and elation, to prove to myself that I am indeed all-in making this company a success.

There's nothing magical in that thinking. It's a mindset you could adopt for yourself right now. Imagine what your life would look like if, instead of dreading the pain and work that achieving whatever it is you're chasing requires, you reveled in it. I don't want to be comfortable. I want to be hungry. I want to be tired. And then I want to do it all again tomorrow. It's only after pushing through all that stuff, and going all-in in a real way, that you can look back and relive those moments when all the hard work bore fruit.

MORE THAN MERE DISCOMFORT

It might be easy to read that passage and think I'm giving the same old advice everyone gives, like some lame life coach telling you to "get out of your comfort zone." What I'm suggesting is more than about making yourself uncomfortable. Going all-in actually suggests the need to seek out hard things, and that being comfortable is actually a condition of being out of your comfort zone.

When things are running smoothly, that worries me. It suggests we aren't pushing hard enough. Problems come with growth, and no problem says to me that we aren't growing, and not growing fills me with more fear than the specter of the next crisis. Everyone around me knows this—I'm happiest when I'm beat down and exhausted from the work, and when the pressure is on.

I remember once, at Fort Benning I was attending an officer's training course, and some captains came over from the Ranger Battalion to teach. A colleague I'd been talking to pointed to one of the captains who he'd worked with in the past. "You see that guy over there?" he said. "That guy is the best when things are fucking nuts. When the shit hits the fan, look over at that guy and he's as cool as the other side of the pillow. The more problems that come up, you'd never know, because the worse it gets, the calmer he gets. He rolls with the punches and makes shit work."

Instantly I knew one thing: I wanted to be just like that guy one day. I don't want to be the guy who loses it when things start falling apart. I want to be the guy who stays calm while everyone else is losing theirs. Going all-in gives you the space to step back in times of crisis, look at the big picture, and begin addressing the obstacles in front of you.

This mindset paid dividends when the company hit (many) speed bumps along the way. As problems arose, especially in the beginning, it would have been so easy to quit, and to see each problem as the end of the world. You have to realize that any new venture has growing pains, but growing pains are good. It means you're growing. You have to see the future, how things will be better in a month, or a year.

Going all-in replaces escape plans with the steely resolve to see your way through to success.

ALL-IN CREATES CHANGE

In the beginning of the company, I thought I could dabble. I tried to think of it first as just this side thing I would try to do. In my naivete, I thought business owners had tons of free time, lots of money, and tons of freedom. I didn't realize that when you start a business, it becomes like your baby. It becomes a part of you. It didn't take me long to realize the foolishness of trying to dabble.

Dabbling isn't going all-in. It's just like dipping your toes in the water rather than jumping in. And as a dabbler, the early results were poor. We didn't progress as a company until I finally said to myself, "I'm going all-in on this shit. I'm making this work, whether I die with it or whatever."

Doing that gave me the fortitude to do whatever I needed to make the company work. There were no excuses I could fall back on. Once I went all-in, anything that wasn't directly related to the success of the company—sleep, food, a life outside the company—became secondary.

Once I did that, things started to change, things started to pay off. I wasn't looking for excuses anymore at that point. People say it takes three years to grow a business. I used to comfort myself with that idea as the company floundered in its first few years, but the reality is that I wasn't all-in, and used the three-year timetable as an excuse for my own failings.

PLANNING

One of the things going all-in does is it brings clarity. You see your situation for what it is, and you're able to solve problems in ways that you might not if you had no skin in the game. Going all-in removes the safety net of Plan B.

There's no looking back. You've made your decision and now it's time to devote every scrap of energy you have into making it a reality.

While before, a little detachment from the business, where I allowed the idea of failure to creep into my mind, would have been my crutch. Once I went all-in, though, failure was no longer an option. My crutch instead became operational planning. There are a lot of decisions I needed to make as I grew the business, and as we grew, the stakes for each of those decisions rose. My way of dealing with those risks is to double down on planning, research, and market evaluation. It's all a way to mitigate risk, make it smaller. There will always be risk in anything you do, but if you implement systems and mitigate that risk, you'll sleep better at night.

I learned a lot of this from my first platoon sergeant, SFC Muniz. He taught me amazing lessons in motivating our people to make the most effective use of the working day, and how to manage time and people. One of the things I learned was delegation. Because he was so strong on the people management side of things, he freed me up to focus on the larger-picture, administrative stuff and other assorted tasks an army lieutenant has to do on any given day. I could have tried to do it all myself, but that would have taken me ten hours a day. Instead, he taught me how to delegate many tasks across several people, allowing us to get far more done in less time than if I'd taken it all on myself.

The other thing I learned was the importance of communication. During our first live-fire exercise, I'd done a poor job of explaining everyone's role to the entire team, so when the dry-fire exercise (iteration before the live round) went down and the "rounds started flying," no one knew what they were meant to be doing. It was a total shit show. I took that lesson with me into the corporate world, too. When I establish a plan, whether it's in the office with my team and staff, or with the athletes we pay and sponsor, or in interactions with our customers, I make absolutely sure that I've done a great job communicating the plan to everyone, and that everyone understands exactly what is going to, or needs to, happen.

MORE THAN A SLOGAN

The thing I dislike about all these sayings and mottos that people post on places like Instagram, the ones that are meant to motivate and inspire, fall short because there's rarely any context to it. People will say, "Step out of your comfort zone and you will be successful." It all sounds good, but in the end, no one knows how to put it to use because there's no context.

Going all-in is the context. For me, I like taking things to the extreme, doing more than simply becoming uncomfortable. Going all-in means transcending discomfort and embracing the idea of bearing any burden, accepting any pain and suffering, whatever it takes to achieve your dream, whether that's to start and build an amazing business, establish yourself in a career, or meet your goals.

These aren't just words painted on a wall. I'd go insane if I didn't put this idea into practice every single day, every single week, and every single month that I go to work. When I go a long period of where nothing hurts, where there's no stress—whether physical or mental—I start to go a little nuts.

That's when I go out and do something. I think a lot of people *think* they know where their limits lie, and they think they know when they're giving their all at something. But until you learn to break the limits of your own mental and physical capabilities, you'll never realize your full potential.

If you don't know where your limits truly are—and believe me, they're a lot further out there than you think—then you don't know how to operate at your 100 percent.

If you don't operate at 100 percent of your capacity, you're not going all the way in.

I'm twenty-nine years old now, and I often reflect on

where and when I've learned certain important things in my life. Many of these lessons were learned in the army, or from the time I spent building my brand. Some were taught by my parents as I grew up.

Going all-in is something I've recently realized came from my mother.

During the writing of this book, she was diagnosed with advanced ovarian cancer, and passed away just six short months later. She was one-of-a-kind, to say the least. She inspired my brother and me, and thousands of people in Central Pennsylvania.

After she passed, I was talking to a friend of hers, who said something I will never forget: "Your mom found her passion very early in life, and she fulfilled that passion every single day until the day that she passed."

She was right. So many people go about their lives just "living." They aren't pursuing a passion. There is nothing that gets them out of bed in the morning except habit. They aren't living lives of passion, they're just living.

My mom was a special education teacher and supervisor. In her early twenties, she decided this would be her life's work. For the next thirty-seven years, she spent her days literally changing lives through the students and families she taught, both in school and as part of the Special Olympics. My mom found her passion early, and she went ALL-IN fulfilling that passion.

She wasn't worried about how long her workdays were, or how far she'd have to travel, or how much money she made. My mom found so much joy and fulfillment changing the lives of others and constantly giving back. She was all-in.

She changed thousands of lives while she was on this earth, and I know she still changes them, even after she is gone.

That being said, GOING ALL-IN is not just about making the kind of money you might have dreamed of making your entire life, or buying your dream home, or driving that super-fast car you always wanted. GOING ALL-IN is about pursuing your life's passion. The thing that fulfills you. The thing that gets you out of bed in the morning, that drives you to be a better person, to change the lives of those around you, and leave an everlasting impact on the world.

WINNING THE DAY BACK

Once you've gone all-in and learned to stretch yourself and find that 100 percent, you can focus on the next piece of the puzzle, which is winning the day back. On the big scoresheet in my mind, every minute I'm asleep puts me further and further behind. I never remember the successes of yesterday, only the challenges of today. In the next chapter we'll discuss winning the day back, and how to use that concept to relentlessly push forward, even when you've been burdened with success.

★

CHAPTER SEVEN

WINNING THE DAY BACK

A day can be powerful.

Think of how many peoples' lives can change in one day, or one moment in time. How many people find the entire course of their lives changed in a single day? Maybe they discovered a new and innovative invention, or intervened in a bad situation, maybe a natural disaster, and saved thousands of lives.

A day can be powerful.

It's not enough to "own the day." That's a great starting point, but I take it one step further. I don't just want to own the day, I want to win it back.

When the company was struggling, I'd wake up angry

because I wasn't satisfied with myself. I knew I had more potential than I was using, and that I wanted to be somewhere bigger, achieve bigger things. I was happy in most ways, but I wasn't satisfied.

To this day, people still ask what motivates me. They want to know what keeps me moving forward, and where do I get my sense of discipline?

Best-selling author Tucker Max said it best: "The only hell I'm afraid of is, when I die, the man I ended up as… meets the man I could have been."

My solution? If you wake up feeling already at a loss, win that day back.

Every day I wake up behind on the scoreboard. Every day I work to end it with a win. And every morning, it begins all over again.

It's no exaggeration to say that a single day can be powerful. Your empire won't be built in a day, but every day that moves you closer to that goal is POWERFUL.

When I say I wake up "behind on the scoreboard," this doesn't mean I wake up sad, lonely, and in the midst of a pity party.

Not at all.

Instead, I wake up with the knowledge of that day's ultimate potential:

I know what one week has the potential to be.

I know what one month has the potential to be.

I know what one year has the potential to be.

I know what one decade has the potential to be.

I know what one life has the potential to be.

When I wake up, I consciously know what needs to be done to keep moving forward, and when I don't, I know enough to focus solely on figuring it out. If you don't focus on winning the day back, you will find yourself at the end of the day in the exact position you were in at the beginning. You'll find yourself WISHING you were somewhere else, doing something better.

Winning the day back is an incredible way to guard yourself from ever resting on your laurels or from becoming complacent. It works when times are good and it works when times are bad.

Even when I'm up, I approach each new day as if I were down.

A great example was several years ago, when we launched a new protein product. We'd been stymied for a while because we didn't have the new warehouse yet, so we hadn't been able to order any new product due to lack of space to store it. My house just no longer had any more room.

As soon as we moved into that first new warehouse, though, tons of space opened up and we were able to take in an inventory of the new product. We spent months hyping it and generating buzz. As soon as the shipment came in, we advertised it on our website and put it to work.

Our hard work and preparation paid off, and that first day we did $40,000 in sales, our best single-day revenue ever (up until that point). It was a heady time. The company was still just the three of us (my brother, my friend, and myself) and we went out that night for a team dinner to celebrate our success. It was easily the highlight of my entire time with the company.

The next morning?

I woke up proud of everything we'd achieved, but aware

that I was already behind on the scoreboard again. It was almost as if the previous day had never happened. On some level, I was still happy and proud of what we'd accomplished, but that was now yesterday, and yesterday is over. The only thing to do was get right back at it and win today back.

HOW TO WIN THE DAY

Winning the day is never an accident. It's based on understanding that we can only live one day at a time, and that winning the day means making the most of this one day. I might die tomorrow and not achieve the next goal, but as long as I'm here today and able to, I'm going to maximize my chances at success by winning right now.

The main trick to winning the day is getting an early start. My goal every day is to get the majority of the day's work done by 12 p.m. That means an early reveille, and immediately trying to knock out as much shit as possible. For example, on the day I'm writing this, I will also be filming YouTube videos, creating social media content, taking care of business administration work, and planning for the next week, month, quarter, and year. Seriously, I spend part of every day planning the next twelve weeks out, at a minimum. This practice was instilled in me through my time in company level leadership in the army. Planning months in advance allows you to establish short-term goals, down to the daily requirements, in order to reach your longer term goals.

The days have emotional highs and lows, and no day is guaranteed. A lot of people will take their time achieving their goals, especially if they're building a brand or a business, which usually takes about three years even under the best of circumstances. To me, though, during those two or three years, I'm going to be busting my ass as hard as I can every day. I'm not in a rush, not exactly, but I'm not sitting around waiting for success, either. Having a mindset that revolves around winning back the day means automatically that you're going to be the type of person who shows up every day and puts in a ton of work. You may not shorten the timeframe for success by doing this, but you almost certainly won't achieve your goals as quickly if you don't.

START BY LEARNING ONE THING PER DAY

In 2016—nearly four years after opening my business—things really started to click. Everyone used to tell me, "It generally takes about three years to see any results from your business." And you know what? I believed them. One hundred percent.

When I first started, I believed that three years in, things would simply work themselves out, and our product would be flying off the shelves.

I'm here to tell you, it may take three years to see success, but it won't happen due to chance or luck.

I realized this during my army rotation in South Korea.

I spent a lot of time there studying and figuring out this mysterious thing called starting a business. I made it an explicit goal of mine to learn at least one new thing every single day. It had to be something completely new to me, whether that means a new way to edit a video, or a new wrinkle in marketing our products, I had to learn one new thing every day. I knew that if I wasn't learning that one new thing, I wasn't growing and getting better.

Even better, I knew that if I could sneak in a couple extra new things a day, bump my volume up to three new things per day, I'd be adding 1,000 skills to my toolbox. Imagine where you'd be a year from now if you added 1,000 new skills to your skillset. How much more valuable would you be as an employee? What heights could you reach? Where might that new knowledge take you?

SOMETIMES DAYS GET BY YOU

It happens. Once in a while a day sneaks by you and you don't win it back. It bothers me, but it happens. I think this is why I struggle so much with going on vacation. Two or three days into any vacation, max, and I begin to get the itch to come back and get to work. Every day I spend away from work causes me to reflect on how much you can actually get done in a given day, and the knowledge that I didn't do anything that day at all is a hard pill to swallow.

BACKWARDS PLANNING

The end state of any day is the sum of things I need to get done within that day. To keep moving forward I need to know my end state for that day, tomorrow, the next day, and most of the week. To make sure I hit all my targets, I've continued to use the military's tried-and-true planning method known as "backwards planning."

Backwards planning begins with the final destination or objective, then marches the timeline backwards toward the starting point, making allowances for how long each task in between will take. For each task, you move your planning clock backwards accordingly.

For me, this has been the most groundbreaking way to ensure success that I've ever shared with my civilian friends and viewers, and it's something I think veterans undervalue in their daily, post-military lives.

Let's look at the launch of a Bare Performance Nutrition product. That launch includes market research, product research, and development (in concert with our manufacturers), testing, flavor approval, production, marketing, and generating buzz around the product, then the launch itself.

You know what happens when we don't backwards plan? Everything goes to shit.

I'm a visual guy, so I still do most of my planning on whiteboards or large pieces of poster board to create my timeline.

On the far right of the board is our objective—in this case, the product launch.

On the far left, where we are today (i.e., the start).

Everything that happens between the left and right borders are the things that need to be completed in order to ensure a successful launch.

I start from the right side (aka, the end outcome), and move leftward as I plan:

1. Email marketing blast and social media campaigns announcing launch (END GOAL)
2. Athletes and ambassadors receive products and start promoting

3. BPN receives product from manufacturer
4. Manufacturer sources ingredients, blends product, bottles product, tests product
5. BPN places order to put product into production
6. Flavor profiles approved
7. Product ingredient testing approved
8. Product ingredient profile selected
9. Product research and development
10. Market Research & Development + Testing
11. New product idea (TODAY)

Thanks to backwards planning, this rollout is a sixteen-week process. Without it, this might take forty weeks. Backwards planning keeps everyone—from product development and marketing to manufacturing and warehouse operations—in sync, and leads to a successful launch.

Backwards planning is a key piece in successfully winning any day back. It gives you a clear view of how much time you need to hit your goals for the day.

I constantly see people stressed out by the number of things they need to accomplish in a day. They become overwhelmed, disorganized, and unaccomplished. Using backwards planning allows you to organize your day from start to finish. You'll be able to see what needs to get done between getting out of bed in the morning and when you crawl back in at the end of the day.

STRUCTURE

All of my days are heavily structured. I don't pencil in standing appointments or anything like that. It's not like "every day from 9 a.m. to 11 a.m. I'm here, then at 12 p.m. I go..." It's not like that at all. I use that end state and backwards planning to get where I need to go, but that planning takes place every single day. I'm flexible in how I provide the structure I need on any given day, but I'm absolutely inflexible about ensuring that structure is in place.

BE READY FOR THE HIGHS AND LOWS

Embrace them. They're inevitable, you might as well get used to them. My days begin with a low. The day is already slipping away from me and I've been awake for only ten minutes. By the time lunch arrives, I've spent the morning blasting my way through that day's work, and I'm starting to feel better about the chances of winning back yet another day.

Let me be clear about this: When I'm awake for only ten minutes, and still feel like the day is beginning to slip away, I'm not losing my shit. I don't freak out because I'm two minutes late getting out the door. I don't need to be first in line for that morning coffee.

Remember that Ranger Battalion officer I saw at Fort

Benning? The one who was as cool as the other side of the pillow no matter what the situation? That's the guy I'm always striving to be, but as the day starts moving forward, so do you. Time does not wait for anyone.

That's, of course, when a manufacturer will call with a huge problem, and they're not going to ship out our next product. Remember, problems are good. Stressors are good. As long as they're helping you learn and grow, stress and problems are great things to have. That's the best part of being an entrepreneur. Some people with regular jobs can go to work and sit at a desk all day, maybe shell out some paperwork. They don't have highs and lows because if they fuck something up, it's not really their fault. They have a boss or a company to blame. When you own your own business, you don't have that luxury. The responsibility always rests with you. I love that deal. The highs and lows are just reminders of the beauty of being an entrepreneur.

In the beginning, my goal was to avoid all failure. I didn't want to waste a penny, or a single resource. I think that's everyone's goal when they're first starting out. No one wants to waste money. I think, though, that as long as you understand that some risk is inevitable, and that along with that risk-taking some waste is going to follow as part of the learning process, you won't live with any regret. I don't regret any of the decisions I made that didn't work out. I won't make those same mistakes again, but I don't carry those past failures with me like a ball and chain.

Part of winning the day back is the mindset that your end state is always going to be you coming out on top. What was it Thomas Edison said, it wasn't that he didn't succeed once until he'd failed 10,000 times first. I don't care if I wake up down on points, as long as I end the day on top.

GO ONE MORE

Winning the day is the basis of an upward trajectory toward what you want, while the final piece of the puzzle is the jet fuel that gets you there. Going one more, never being satisfied with what you've done, never stopping with the minimum, that's the key to getting where you want to be.

——— ★ ———

CHAPTER EIGHT

GO ONE MORE

Ranger School is sixty-one days long, a gut check marked by little food, less sleep, and huge portions of suck. I was 120 days into it when I first had the idea of going one more. For a guy who loves to wear himself out, you'd think an extended stay in a place like that would be heaven, but I have to admit, even for a guy like me, it was a bit much.

I'd been there so long and after a while it seemed like it might never end. I knew that the usual adaptations we make for the tough times weren't going to be enough. I was depleted, mind and body, and I knew I needed something more to get me to the end. For reasons that are unclear—I was in a fog and simply trying to survive—I adopted this idea of going one more. I know it seems a little vague. One more? One more what?

One more *whatever it takes*. It might mean one more step in the mountains of Georgia or swamps of Florida with a hundred pounds on my back. One more sleepless night editing YouTube footage. One more rep in the weight room. Whatever it takes to get one more step closer to your goal.

Let me put it into some context so you understand where I'm coming from on this one.

We were sitting in a patrol base one morning during the Florida phase. During the mornings, you received your mission brief for the day and the assigned leadership started planning routes, actions on the objective, evacuation plans, and every part of operational planning from patrol base to patrol base. The mornings and evenings were two different types of exhaustion. If you held a leadership role for the day, you were working your ass off to "get your GO," meaning you could move on to the next phase—or in this case, graduate.

I was in leadership this day as a squad leader, and guys were absolutely sucking. Dudes were falling asleep while in security, half-assing sector sketches and skipping routine maintenance on their weapons (which the Ranger instructors were bound to spot check).

The night prior was a rough one. We arrived to our patrol

base around 3 a.m., set up security and were ready to bed down for the night. Unfortunately, someone in the platoon pissed off one of the Ranger instructors and within five minutes of closing my eyes, we were getting hit with artillery simulators and throwing our rucks back on our backs, ready to walk, again.

That walk ended at 5:30 a.m., just in time for the next day to start.

As I tried to motivate my squad, ensuring they were taking notes on the day's mission and topping off all water sources, one of the guys turned to me and said, "I can't do this anymore."

He was about to get kicked out of Ranger School for a L.O.M. (lack of motivation). You can also leave the school whenever you want. You just have to tell the instructors you have a "lack of motivation" to finish.

I told him, "Come on man, just go one more day. Tomorrow will be better."

The truth, however, was that the next day would probably be worse, but I wanted to persuade this guy to take it day by day.

One day at a time.

Just to go ONE MORE.

Everyday.

Until you graduate.

And that is what he and many others did.

It's a powerful way of thinking, and you can put it to use, too.

In the civilian world, going one more helped get me through my second marathon. For the first one, I'd trained with a hat with "embrace the suck" on the bill. I always train in a hat, and I'd had that slogan put on there for motivation. The next year I wrote "One More" on the inside of the bill.

I shared a photo of the picture on the company YouTube channel, and it took off. For the next three months, thousands of people reached out to us to show us pictures of their own hats with the words "One More" scrawled on the bill. It started a small movement. Clearly we'd touched on a nerve.

That movement started on a training run that nearly went bad.

I'd planned to go eighteen miles that day. I was about a month out from the marathon. Early in the run, I could tell it wasn't my day. I was sucking, big time. One thing about me is that, on off days like that, I tend to get angry with myself. My solution is to step outside of myself and, like the old cartoon with the angel on the shoulder whispering in my ear, willing me on. Of course, this angel isn't all light and sunshine.

If I'm running and just not feeling it that day, thoughts creep into my head: "I should stop for the day." "Today is not my day."

That's when the angel pipes up, "Shut the fuck up, Nick. Drive through this."

On this day, my moment of truth came at about mile ten. My legs were heavy and I wasn't sure I had it in me to finish the final eight miles. The angel had a plan, though. "Shut the fuck up, Nick. We're going to go nineteen miles today!" The angel's solution was to go one more mile, just to prove I had it in me to do what I'd said I'd do, and then some.

And that's exactly what I did. On a day when everything inside me begged to quit, when I didn't think I had the goods to do all eighteen miles, I pushed myself to not only finish, but to go further than I thought I could.

BREAKING BARRIERS

That's what "go one more" is all about, and, to be honest, the main idea of this entire book. Tap into the power of pushing yourself to break past the physical and mental barriers that separate you from where you are and where you want to be.

So many people limit their chances for achievement by jumping into projects or a workout or anything in life and work limited by what they think are their possibilities. They have expectations about the limits of their mental and physical performance. These expectations are almost always far less than what they could actually accomplish if they pushed themselves. Going one more is a natural way to push past those self-imposed limits and let your mind and body work to their full potential.

Push back against those barriers. Those are walls we build before we start anything. Before starting a business. Before going on a workout. Before starting a new job. It's natural to want to protect yourself by setting limits that you can easily bump up against. This gives you the false impression of really working to your capacity. In reality, it just means you're working within your comfort zone.

Going one more is about stretching limits. It should hurt. It should not feel easy or comfortable. Find what you think is your limit, then go beyond it. Believe me, when you find yourself at mile nineteen, whether figuratively or literally, it'll be one of the greatest moments of your life.

BREAKING DOWN EXPECTATIONS

At its simplest, the idea is to go one step beyond the line you've drawn for yourself. Another way to look at it is, the moment you start making excuses for yourself, for not meeting a goal or for not hitting your end state for the day, things I call "tiny heart moments," that's when you need to make the conscious decision to not only do what you said you were going to do, but to go one more.

Let me explain what these "tiny heart moments" (also known as "tiny heart syndrome") are all about. When I was in ROTC at the Indiana University of Pennsylvania, and getting ready to commission into the US Army, we had an instructor who I will always remember. Master Sergeant Ortega was one of the first people I met who taught me how to "go one more."

He dragged me through my first twelve-mile ruck march while I carried a fifty-pound pack, forced me to run endless sprints up an old ski mountain, push water cans uphill while low-crawling, and put my body through a world of hurt.

I fucking loved all of it.

MSG Ortega would take us on long workouts and push us until someone began looking to quit. They'd be falling out of the run and Ortega would use the opportunity to talk about "tiny heart syndrome." He said it's a self-induced disease caused by an individual allowing their body to control their mind and their forward movement.

Greatness doesn't come from people with tiny hearts, those folks who run up against obstacles and struggles, then turn around and walk the other way.

If you're on a run and it's supposed to be a ten-miler, and your mind and body begin making excuses to quit at mile seven, you need to recognize that for what it is: BS. It's also a compromise, and if you're really all-in and committed to seeing this thing through, no matter what it is, compromise is a four-letter word.

So instead of completing those ten miles (and patting yourself on the back for sticking with it), you need to embrace the idea of going eleven. The benefits you'll gain from that extra six to ten minutes of effort (depending on your exhaustion and normal pace) will far exceed the work you put in.

This has implications for your broader life, too. Imagine if you put in one more day of work. Or one more week pushing to start your business. One more year of going balls to the wall to make your dream job work?

No matter whether it's a set in the weight room, or starting a business, or going to a school in the military, people tend to go into these things with expectations. Those expectations are often based on fear, or false beliefs about the limits of their own potential. Going one more is about erasing those limits and helping people realize they're capable of far more than their minds and bodies are telling them. You can always do one more rep. What you think failure is, is not failure. You can fail more. You can fail better.

The trick is to get outside of your own head, especially when things get tough. I used to think of it as if I had a clone of myself, and when things got really bad, that clone would push me harder. It was sort of like kicking my own ass. You've got to go external and see the situation for what it is, not what it *feels like*. Like I said earlier in the book, the body is merely an accessory to your mind, not the other way around. If you can go external and pull yourself away from that inner struggle, you'll find yourself achieving things you never thought possible.

IT'S NOT WHAT YOU WANT, IT'S HOW BADLY YOU WANT IT

I remember growing up filled with envy for other peoples' lives. I'd look at people I admired and wish my life was like theirs. Of course, this would be followed by some defeatist shit like, "I can't be like them because I'm me, and not them." It was a weird logic, but it reflected the barriers I'd erected around my own success, even at a young age.

As I got older, I began to realize the only thing separating me from what I wanted was how badly I wanted it. I came to understand that literally anything I wanted was at my fingertips, I just have to go after it. It might take a day, it might take a week, it might take years, but regardless, it's right there for the taking.

The question is how badly do I want it? What am I willing to sacrifice to get it?

The effect is compounding. Critics might say, "Running one more mile isn't really going to offer that much improvement." OK, true. But that's only if you look at the one individual workout. Compound that extra mile over a year's worth of workouts, and then what have you got?

It's never just one thing. Go one more once, keep it up and the next thing you know you've gone one more 1,000 times, then those thousand things turn into 10,000, and before you know it, you've broken through every barrier you've ever imposed on yourself. People will be amazed at your success and want to know your secret. They probably won't believe that it's something so simple as putting in that one extra unit of work. Good. Less competition for you.

It's a lot like compounding interest on investments. You put $10,000 in the bank at today's lousy interest rates, and over time, you'll still have that $10,000 and not much more. Invest that same money in the stock market or a mutual fund, though, and over that same time, thanks to the miracle of compounding interest, you could turn that $10,000 into $100,000 in the same amount of time (or lose it all, I suppose; that's why we mitigate risk by doing our research).

Applying the go one more mentality to everyday life will have similar results. Take the example from the last chapter of learning one new thing every day. Taken individually, not all these new things are going to be super important, but collectively, after a year or two and you've added hundreds, if not a thousand, new skills to your toolbox, that's an amazing compounding effect. Those 1,000 more skills will make you 1,000 times better than you were before.

IT'S WORKING

I see the results of this little movement every day in the people who reach out to us, especially on social media, to say that going one more has changed their lives. We get

DMs and emails every day from people who've adopted the mentality and are seeing results they never thought possible. I have hundreds and hundreds of pictures people have sent with "One More" written on the bills of their hats.

It's helped a lot of people. I hear success stories all the time of people who've put One More to use to reach fitness goals, or working toward their dream job, or starting a business. It's helped a lot of people, and I hope anyone reading this book will give it a try, too. We're trained as children and then into adulthood to crave comfort and to avoid pain. It's a mindset that hampers us because it means we're never working at capacity. We're definitely not exceeding capacity, which anyone who's involved with fitness can tell you is the secret sauce to getting stronger. Our minds have the ability to adapt the same way our muscles adapt and grow stronger due to repetitive stresses placed on them.

BUT WHAT ABOUT BURNOUT?

I can't tell you how many times I've been told, "I don't want to burn out," or, "I don't want to overdo it." We live in a world where so many people are AFRAID of doing too much. If you are AFRAID of doing too much, accomplishing too much, pushing yourself too hard and getting everything you ever dreamed of out of life, then what the hell are you doing reading this book?

This way of living is not for everyone. Not everyone wants MORE or BETTER. To each their own. Me? I want to push my mind, my body, my possibilities, above and beyond anything I ever thought possible. I want to cross the finish line to my Ironman race and collapse in exhaustion. I want to spend late nights trying to figure out how to take Bare Performance Nutrition to the next level, and I want to push my body to feel fatigue and muscle failure. I live for it.

I've been burnt out and I've been over-trained. I know where my 100 percent lies. It doesn't feel good and it takes a LOT to get there.

OVER-TRAINING DOES EXIST

In 2017, I decided to add a lot to my plate. In addition to building my supplement company and creating content for YouTube as I transitioned out of the military, I decided to challenge myself. I added two to three Cross-Fit workouts a day to my routine and began training for my first marathon, a race in Austin, Texas. I continued daily bodybuilding training throughout.

I'll admit it. It was one of the dumbest things I've ever done, and I was bound to over-train.

I endured this routine for three months. I got very little sleep and ran my body into the ground.

Eventually, I hit the wall.

I found myself unable to get through a workout without stopping for multiple rests. My motivation was at absolute zero (although despite this, I kept going). My body stopped recovering and everything hurt. I couldn't sleep and, the cherry on the top, my ability to have sex with my now-fiancé was nonexistent.

My body was as limp as it gets, and I learned my lesson.

This was not the first time I'd reached my personal 100 percent, but it was the first time it had happened as a civilian, and it hit me harder.

I tell you this because as much as it feels good to push yourself, it feels good to find out what you're capable of, and what you can accomplish with all that training. Just know when you've gone too far.

And if you're wondering, yes, I did recover from all my "underperforming," and one side effect of pushing yourself that hard is that, once you recover, every other workout seems easier.

GO ONE MORE

It's that simple. It's where I came up with the title for this book. May your days be so full that you cram twenty-five hours of work and play into the day. Go one more.

Whatever you think is your limit, go one more. Whenever you think you've done all you can do, do one more. Forget the haters. Move forward and let the things you've learned build upon each other, compounding their effects on your growth and success. Look for that moment when you're feeling your weakest. Somewhere in there is the key to breaking through and becoming whatever it is you want to be in life.

CONCLUSION

My story began on a small dairy farm in Pennsylvania, and in a lot of ways I'm still that regular kid who believes in hard work and old-fashioned traits like discipline and integrity. But I'm also a Ranger-tabbed army veteran who regularly pushes himself beyond his physical and mental limits, both in fitness and business, in the passionate pursuit of success.

In short, I'm just like you.

I hope this book has given you an idea of what my journey has been, and hope for what yours may become. I don't have any hacks or shortcuts to offer, but I do have some principles.

NEXT STEPS

The secret of success is that there's no secret. The first step? Recognize that growth is always going to include pain and discomfort. That's what stretching will do. The first thing you need to do, then, is to lean into the most painful and difficult parts of your journey. Embrace the suck. Welcome the pain and the exhaustion—mental and physical—as a sign that you're working toward something worth the effort.

How did I survive 141 days in Ranger School, double the usual time a candidate spends in one of the military's most grueling courses? The first thing I did was embrace the pain and misery, the weariness and hunger, and by doing that found a way to transcend it all.

Next, understand that nothing truly worth doing is going to be easy. Like my father always said, if it were easy, anyone could do it. Remind yourself of this when the struggles come, and they will. The difficulties mean you've chosen to do something special, something worth the time and effort.

Understanding this will get you through the inevitable tough times. And I know it's something of a theme with me, but remember: tough times are coming. Without a doubt. The thing that separates truly successful people from everyone else is the ability to not only persevere through tough times, but to be able to actually thrive during them.

One of the main tools to surviving tough times and kicking ass when things are good is to build on your knowledge and capabilities every day. I call it becoming a "learning machine," someone who's constantly adding to their toolbox of skills and knowledge. Especially in the beginning of a new business, when money is tight or, in our case, nonexistent, the ability to tap into the vast information available online these days and to teach yourself the skills and techniques that will push you to the next level is priceless.

Avoid self-pity, or anything that reeks of feelings of entitlement. Remember always that none of us are owed a damn thing. If you wait for someone to give you the things you think you deserve, you'll be waiting for a day that will never arrive. Don't wait. Get to work. Bust your ass as if nothing is guaranteed, because you're right. There are no free lunches and no guarantees.

Commit and be relentless in anything you pursue. Going all-in will give you the laser focus and clarity to see what it is you really need to do to achieve your dreams. Limit distractions. Cut out nonsense. Focus. Do not be afraid to sacrifice. Your goal is worth it, why settle for anything less than total effort?

GO ALL-IN

Most importantly, I hope this book has shown you what passion and commitment can do for you. Throw yourself into everything you do. Follow your passions, and commit to them totally. Shortcuts are traps—be suspicious of anything easy.

As you go forward in your journey toward finding that twenty-five hours in a day, I'd love to keep in touch. You can follow me and Bare Performance Nutrition on YouTube simply by searching "Nick Bare," or Instagram @ nickbarefitness. Let us know how you're doing. Share your journey and be the inspiration you seek!

ACKNOWLEDGMENTS

I have to start by thanking my amazing fiancé, Stefany. From supporting my ambitious drive and actions to inspiring me as I watch you inspire others.

To my dad: I can never thank you enough for all the valuable lessons you taught me as I grew up. Your selfless character and hard work have left a massive impact on me. I'll never forget the words, "If it were that easy, everyone would do it."

To my brother, Preston: I could never have done any of this without you. You moved to Texas when I needed help with Bare Performance Nutrition, and you have put in just as many hours as I have. This company is just as much yours as it is mine.

To the soldiers and NCOs of 1st Platoon, Bravo Company, 2-12: I knew that joining the military would provide me a great experience with valuable lessons, but I never realized how much it would change my life. I learned so much from all of you and enjoyed every waking minute, whether we were running miles through Fort Hood, playing pranks on 1LT Pedersen's platoon, sleeping in the back of the Bradley's, or training throughout the nights. MISFITS.

To the Bare Performance Nutrition team, family, customers, and viewers: Thank you for being a part of the journey that is just getting started, thank you for believing in the vision that we have created, and thank you for all of your support over the years.

You mean the world to us.

ABOUT THE AUTHOR

NICK BARE is the owner and founder of Bare Performance Nutrition, a premier source of the best sports and nutritional supplements on the market today. A former lieutenant in the US Army and graduate of Ranger School, one of the most physically and mentally grueling tests in the world, Nick continues to seek the most compelling challenges he can in his quest for self-improvement and achievement. Through his social media presence, Nick has become an ambassador to anyone looking to improve their lives through fitness and mental strength. He lives and works in Austin, Texas.

www.bareperformancenutrition.com